S. V. SLAVIN

THE SOVIET NORTH

Present Development and Prospects

Progress Publishers
Moscow

Translated from the Russian by Don Danemanis

С. В. Славин
ОСВОЕНИЕ СЕВЕРА СОВЕТСКОГО СОЮЗА
На английском языке

First printing 1972

Printed in the Union of Soviet Socialist Republics

CONTENTS

Preface 5

Development of the North—a World Trend 7

Chapter One. THE HISTORICAL BACKGROUND 13

Chapter Two. THE NORTH IN THE SOVIET ECONOMY 38

Chapter Three. ASPECTS OF DEVELOPMENT 58

Chapter Four. THE IMPROVEMENT OF ECONOMIC
EFFICIENCY 80

Chapter Five. THE EUROPEAN NORTH 92

Chapter Six. THE SIBERIAN NORTH 129

Chapter Seven. NORTH-EAST USSR 149

A Look Into the Future 182

PREFACE

The long-standing campaign to develop the Soviet Union's cold, sparsely populated northern territories and to tap their immeasurable resources has gained fresh impetus in recent years. It is sufficient to note that between 1960 and 1970 twice as much money was allocated to the economic development of the northern territories as had been allocated during the more than 40 years of the Soviet Union's existence prior to 1960. The plans for the development of the Soviet Union's economy are now indissolubly linked with the programme for the development of the North.

This book describes the process of exploitation of the country's northern regions and the growth of their productive capacity. It outlines the prospects held out by the economic advance of the North, both those which are presently visible and those more distant, which may be forecast, and their importance to the Soviet Union's economy.

The book is based on the author's monograph *The Development of Industry and Transport in the Soviet North*, published in 1961 by the "Ekonomika" Publishing House in Moscow in Russian. This edition has been greatly supplemented and amended; some material of a narrowly specialised character has been omitted.

DEVELOPMENT
OF THE NORTH—A WORLD TREND

The development of the northern regions of our planet and of the Arctic Ocean, through whose icefields mankind has for centuries endeavoured to establish a shipping route, is one of man's most exciting adventures. History is rich for the courageous exploits of explorers and scholars who penetrated to these remote regions by land and by sea, challenged the raging elements and battled alone with them in their search for a route through the Arctic Ocean.

In the past the North mainly attracted merchants, who bought valuable furs from the natives cheaply, and people who, during the "gold rush", were drawn there by a vision of wealth, ignored the dangers and often paid with their lives for their daring. A vivid picture of the initial conquest of America's rich but highly inaccessible North has been drawn by Jack London, who described man's bitter struggle against the elements.

Those times are long past. The North has changed, as have the problems it presents, and the methods and techniques needed for its development, but the endeavours to tap its natural wealth grow more determined as time goes by. Man creates ever new and ever more perfect means of subduing cruel Nature.

What explains this general movement to the North, to parts of the world where man finds it difficult to live? The shift from areas with more favourable to areas with less favourable climatic conditions is explained by the fact that the resources of the North are needed for further economic development. The pace and the scale of this development are determined by the economic advantages to be obtained from bringing these resources into production.

The economic growth rates of different countries diverge at each stage of their development. Even though development rates fluctuate, a look at the dynamics of world production over the centuries clearly shows that its scale has been constantly increasing and has become truly gigantic in recent decades. According to forecasts this growth will continue during our century and beyond it. The growth of production demands a constant increase in the output and utilisation of the basic raw materials, fuel and power, which are hidden in the bowels of the earth or are found on its surface, in the seas, oceans, rivers and lakes.

Even though the progress of science and technology has made it possible to lower the specific outlay of raw materials and power per unit of finished output, the rate of extraction of natural resources is steadily increasing. Thus, the average yearly increase in the rate of extraction of basic minerals, expressed in terms of value, was 1.2 per cent in the 18th century; about 4 per cent in the 19th-20th centuries (up to 1910 when it dropped somewhat), rose to 5.6 per cent between 1950 and 1964, and reached 6.4 per cent in 1964. If it continues to grow without interruption, the rate of mineral extraction will, by the year 2000, have increased 13.5 times as compared with 1950, while it increased only 3.5 times during the first half of our century.

The vast increase in the quantity of natural resources consumed can be seen from the following comparative data on the USA and the USSR. The average yearly growth rate in the consumption of natural resources between 1913 and 1940 was 1.5 per cent in the USA and 2.5 per cent in the USSR; between 1940 and 1960 it was correspondingly 1.9 and 2.8 per cent. The total quantity of natural resources consumed grew between 1913 and 1960 almost threefold in the USA and sevenfold in the USSR. The figures for the consumption of specific natural] resources in the world at large and in the biggest countries are even more spectacular.

In the USSR the output of coal increased between 1913 and 1969 21 times, that of oil—32 times and of iron ore—20 times. Extraction of natural gas, started in 1928 (300 million cu. m.), had risen 60 times by 1969. These figures greatly exceed the average increase in the rate of extraction of these resources in the world as a whole.

Naturally, this makes it necessary to prospect for new raw material and power resources and to develop them.

World Extraction of Minerals

	1913	1967	Increment (1967 as compared with 1913, number of times)
Oil, mln. tons	56.0	1,758.7	31.4
Natural gas, '000 mln. cu. m.	—	822.4	—
Coal, mln. tons	1,341.6	2,642.0	2.0
Iron ore, mln. tons	176.5	339.8	1.9
Polymetallic ores (according to metal content, '000 tons):			
Bauxites	537.1	46,350.0	86.3
Copper	1,008.1	5,010.0	5.0
Lead	1,201.7	2,950.0	2.4
Zinc	1,024.5	4,850.0	4.7
Nickel	32.5	477.0	14.9

However, raw materials and power extracted from the ground are unrenewable; oil, natural gas, ore and other minerals were formed and accumulated in the course of many ages. The exhaustion of reserves in relatively accessible areas makes it necessary to seek them further away.

In recent decades the extraction of oil from the bottom of the sea has begun, and this oil now accounts for a large part of the world's total production. It is planned to extract natural gas from the bottom of the North Sea and supply Britain with it. The USSR is extracting oil from the Caspian seabed. It was found that the sea-shelves in many countries contain a wealth, not only of oil and natural gas, but also of many highly concentrated minerals, which it would be economic to process. Plans are being made to extract minerals from the upper mantle, lying under the earth's crust. To do this it would be necessary to penetrate dozens of kilometres below the surface. It has been found that there are vast deposits of various minerals on the ocean floor; they have been estimated to exceed the known dry-land reserves but their extraction would involve working under water many kilometres deep.

With the advance of science and technology it is not the remoteness of the deposits or even the technical difficulties that have to be contended with to tap them that decide whether they will be developed or not, but the economic advantages offered by their development and utilisation, that is, a thorough calculation is made of the total requisite outlay and the probable returns. Within the next 15-20 years preference will probably be given to the utilisation of deposits lying relatively close to the surface, among which, in particular, are the vast and as yet untapped resources of the North, the deserts and semideserts.

Investigation has shown that the ore in many northern deposits, lying at distances of thousands of kilometres from the economically developed countries and regions, contains more valuable elements and is found in more accessible seams than in identical deposits in less remote latitudes, and that it is therefore more profitable to tap these deposits even though the difficulties connected with their exploitation require additional outlay. The northern deposits frequently contain natural resources in short supply, which are of great importance to the country's economic development or form a valuable export commodity. These considerations, in fact, dictate the choice of new development projects.

In the context of an enormous, world-wide growth in the rate of production the sharp increase in the consumption of some raw materials has meant that their reserves are being quickly exhausted. This applies primarily to oil and gas, which are not only cheap fuels but also valuable raw materials for the chemical industry, now playing a major role in the economies of all developed countries. Thus, at the present rate of extraction, the known oil reserves of the USA will last for only another 10-12 years. Some minerals, such as gold, tin, diamonds, non-ferrous metals and rare elements, as well as raw materials for the production of light metals, which are particularly important in our time, and heat-resisting substances, etc., are comparatively rare and have to be extracted even in regions that are difficult of access.

Many of the minerals urgently needed in the modern world are concentrated in the northern regions and the southern deserts and semideserts. Thus, the richest diamond-fields are found in South Africa and in North Yakutia while the largest reserves of oil and gas lie in the deserts of the South and in the North. Deposits of non-ferrous metals, raw materials for the production of aluminium and enormous reserves of water power are concentrated in the northern regions.

Many capitalist countries did not develop the natural resources of the North for a long time because of the inflow of cheap raw materials and fuel from African, Asian and Latin American countries. The situation changed in the post-war years, when most of these countries freed themselves of colonialist oppression. Under altered conditions it became more profitable for many big capitalist countries, including the USA, to develop and exploit the natural wealth of their own northern regions. In this context plans are being made for the development of many areas in North Canada, Alaska and the Scandinavian countries. This shows clearly the general trend towards the utilisation of the natural wealth of the North.

In contrast with many economically developed capitalist countries, the Soviet Union has always used domestic raw materials and fuel to supply its expanding industry. The Soviet North has been developing at an increasing rate as a result of the concentration there of vast natural wealth, which is either absent in other parts of the country or available in insufficient quantities. Consequently, the exploitation of the northern resources is vitally important for the rapidly growing Soviet economy. This, in fact, explains the attention devoted to intensive development of the Soviet Union's northern regions, which has in recent years assumed unprecedented proportions.

CHAPTER ONE
THE HISTORICAL BACKGROUND

The history of the exploration and economic development of the North of the Soviet Union and of other countries contains many exciting chapters. We may read of the courage and daring of explorers, of the arduous toil demanded of the people working in the North, of their constant struggle against cruel Nature. But it is not the purpose of this book to recount a vast body of historical facts. We shall therefore give only a short description of the development of Russia's North during the past hundred years or so, embracing the capitalist epoch up to the October Revolution and the Soviet period.

The Development
of the North Under Capitalism

Russia embarked on capitalist development much later than the West European countries. To preserve her independence and sovereignty, she was obliged to develop her own industry and create a network of railways, without which an advance of the country's economy was inconceivable. The building of railways and of many industrial projects was financed by the state.

Most of the railways that existed before the October Revolution were built between 1870 and 1910 (58,500 of the total length of 72,000 versts[1] that existed by 1917); the rate of construction was particularly high between 1890

---

[1] Verst—Russian linear measure of 1.0668 km.—*Ed.*

and 1900 (23,600 versts). The dimensions assumed by road construction demanded considerable development of the iron and steel, coal-mining and other branches of heavy industry, and subsequently also of light industry.

Industry was located mainly in the central and southern parts of European Russia, where a large section of the population was concentrated. The vast borderlands of the Russian Empire, whose area was several times larger than that of the metropolitan region, were internal colonies—sources of cheap raw materials and markets for the sale of the industrial goods produced in the central parts of the country. The development of new areas was largely confined to the rich farming lands in the south-east of the country's European part and in southern Siberia.

Severe climatic conditions and other reasons prevented the agricultural development of the northern borderlands at that time. The Russian capitalists could not exploit the natural wealth of the North because there was no transport to link it with the central industrial regions, there were no roads, and the land was sparsely populated. The development of the North required huge capital investment while at the same time, as compared with the populated regions of the country, a much longer period was needed to recoup this investment. In the North, and especially in the Asiatic part, only Russian trading firms operated. Because of the great difficulty involved in delivering goods to these remote trackless areas and because this required considerable capital outlay, all trade with the native population of northern Siberia came to be controlled by a closed group of merchants, who had an extensive network of agents among the local population. They made huge profits by selling the goods the northern people wanted for their economic activities and everyday life at exorbitant prices and by buying up valuable furs cheaply. Their greatest source of income was the sale of alcohol. To increase their profits the merchants brought the hunters and reindeer breeders under their control by granting them extensive credit.

The western and eastern territories of Russia's North, which are located near sea routes, had long attracted the attention of foreign entrepreneurs. They exploited the rich forests in Arkhangelsk Gubernia and engaged in whaling, sealing, fishing and in trade with the local population on the Okhotsk, Kamchatka and Chukotka coasts. Foreigners controlled the route to Siberia through the Kara Sea and the outlets of the Ob and Yenisei rivers. Foreign capitalists often carried on their activities under the Russian flag, using Russian entrepreneurs as intermediaries. The tsarist government encouraged the expansion of foreign activity in Russia's North.

To give a clearer picture of the economic development of Russia's North under capitalism, we shall discuss at greater length the economic development of the European North, the problem of opening up a sea route to Siberia, specific details concerning the expansion of foreign capital in Russia's North-East and a number of other questions.

The territory of pre-revolutionary Russia's European North embraced the Arkhangelsk, Olonets and part of the Vologda gubernias (that is, Murmansk and Arkhangelsk regions and the Karelian and Komi Autonomous republics according to the present administrative division). In the latter half of the 19th century the coastal population engaged mainly in fishing. With the development of capitalism in Russia at the turn of the century forestry, saw-milling and wood-tar distillation began to play an important part in the economy of Arkhangelsk Gubernia. These branches of industry were rapidly developing.

Before the building of the Vologda-Arkhangelsk railway (in 1898) foreign capital was dominant in the timber industry in the European North. After the railway had been built, Russian capital penetrated into the timber industry of Arkhangelsk Gubernia, although foreign capitalists continued to exert considerable influence. Thus, in 1914, fifty per cent of the timber mills in Arkhangelsk and all the mills in the areas around Lake Onega and in the Pechora basin were foreign-owned. The mills of Russian entrepreneurs (and the forestry industry as a whole) depended on foreign capital. Foreign firms completely controlled the export trade. In 1913 practically all the timber milled was exported to Western Europe (chiefly to England) and only a negligible proportion (2,300 tons) went to Russia's central regions.

The number of timber mills grew from nine in 1861 to forty-four in 1913, while the export of timber grew from 454,000 tons in 1900 to 1,440,000 tons in 1913. Timber was cut mainly in the valleys of the Northern Dvina and the Onega, whence it could most easily be sent to the White Sea ports.

The timber industry yielded high profits—an average of 34 per cent. Some firms were earning over 60 per cent on invested capital.

Salt manufacture and the mining of grinding stone were promoted in Arkhangelsk Gubernia. There were also several minute iron and steel works, using ore found in local bogs, while a few small foundries and copper-smelting plants had long operated in the Povenets district of the Olonets gubernia. Later, when the Ukrainian and Ural metal industries, which provided cheaper metal, had developed, these factories were closed. Shipbuilding had been carried on since the 16th century in some coastal areas (Arkhangelsk, Kem, Kolva, Mezen and Onega).

Arkhangelsk had long been the centre for foreign trade in European Russia's North. In the latter half of the 19th century timber, tar, flax, flax seed, ropes and strings were exported via Arkhangelsk; after the building in 1899 of the Perm-Kotlas railway Siberian grain was also exported.

Codfish, haddock and salmon were caught mainly near the coasts of the Kola Peninsula. Russian ships caught only between 300,000-400,000 poods[1] a year, while the Norwegians, Swedes, British and others caught millions of poods of fish in Russia's northern waters, which they processed and later re-exported to Russia. Large quantities of Norwegian herring were sold at the autumn fairs in Arkhangelsk. Foreigners also actively engaged in the hunting of whales and seals.

The building of railways linking the European North with the country's central regions was vitally important to the economic development of the former. However, it was begun much later there than in other parts of the country. The railways were built in the European North with state capital. Although their building was prompted at that time mainly by strategic considerations, they began later to play an important economic role. Among them were the Vologda-Arkhangelsk railway, which was built between 1894 and 1898 as a narrow-gauge railway and in 1916, that is towards the end of the First World War, was converted to a wide-gauge track, and the Petrozavodsk-Murmansk railway, which was completed in the same year. Military

---

[1] Pood—Russian measure of weight of 16.381 kg or 0.16380496 metric tons.—*Ed.*

Д Е К Р Е Т   пр. № 644 п. 2?

1. В целях всестороннего и планомерного исследования Северных морей, их островов, побережий, имеющих в настоящее время Государственно-важное значение, учредить при Народном Комиссариате Просвещения Плавучий Морской Научный Институт с отделениями; биологическим, гидрологическим, метеорологическим и геологическо-минералогическим.

2. Организованный при НК Просвещения Плавучий Морской Биологический Институт ввести в состав учрежденного настоящим декретом Института в качестве его биологического отделения.

3. Положение об Институте поручить разработать Наркомпросу по соглашению с Морским ведомством и В.С.Н.Х.

4.- Районом деятельности Института определить Северный Ледовитый океан с его морями и устьями рек, островами и прилегающими к нему побережьями Р.С.Ф.С.Р. Европы и Азии.

5. Поручить соответствующим учреждениям снабжение Института углем, жидким топливом, оборудованием и продовольствием наравне с учреждениями первостепенной государственной важности.

6. Установление норм снабжения продовольствием ученного состава Института возложить на Комиссию по Снабжению рабочих при Народном Комиссариате Продовольствия.-

Председатель Совета
Народных Комиссаров

Управляющий Делами Совета
Народных Комиссаров

С е к р е т а р ь

Москва - Кремль
10/III-21 г.

Lenin's decree on the Plavmornin

The Kola tundra in May

Apatite ore from the Tsentralny mine on the Rasvumchorr mountain

The Rasvumchorr mountain on the Kola Peninsula. It contains
a wealth of apatite ore

Evenk women riding reindeers

Skiers training near Syktyvkar, the capital of the Komi ASSR

A Russian language lesson at a school in the village of Lovozero in the central part of the Kola Peninsula, inhabited by Saamis

Members of the Nenets Youth Company of Naryan-Mar dancing the Podarok (Gift), a national dance

After a shopping tour at the department store

The Arkhangelsk port. The ship Sayanyles is taking on cargo

Reindeer herds grazing in the tundra

equipment and a variety of goods for the army and the population were imported through Arkhangelsk. The export of goods from Russia via that port also increased steadily. During the First World War imports through Arkhangelsk increased by more than 260 times in terms of value (from 5.1 to 1,329 million rubles) while exports increased by more than eight times (from 32.4 to 258.1 million rubles). The Petrozavodsk-Murmansk railway gave access to the ice-free port of Murmansk. The Perm-Kotlas railway, the only one without military significance, provided, through Arkhangelsk, the shortest route for Siberian grain exports.

* * *

The development of the Northern Sea Route to Siberia represented one of Russia's greatest problems. As a result of over-population in the black-earth regions of European Russia, large numbers of peasants migrated in the 1880s to Siberia. Agriculture became one of the main economic activities. The building in the nineties of the Trans-Siberian Railway considerably increased the number of immigrants and increased agricultural production in Siberia. However, Siberian grain could not compete with grain grown in European Russia, which was several thousand kilometres closer to the Baltic grain-exporting ports. To hinder the export of Siberian grain to the world markets, the landowners from the European part of the country succeeded in having the tariff rebates granted for long-distance transport to Siberian grain-growers cancelled. As a result of the rise in haulage costs the Siberian peasant was frequently unable to recoup the expenditure involved in producing his grain. An average 100-150 million poods of unmarketable surplus grain accumulated every year in Siberia.

The consequent distribution crisis arrested the development of Siberia's agriculture and compelled many peasants to return to European Russia. Thus, in 1910 the number of people returning to the central regions comprised 36 per cent, and in 1911, 60 per cent of the total of immigrants to Siberia during that time.

A sea route through the Kara Sea from the outlets of the Ob and Yenisei would have provided a comparatively cheap way to export Siberian grain to the world markets. By that route transport costs (32 kopeks per pood at the then

prevailing prices) would have been less than half those incurred by sending the grain to the Baltic ports by railway.
The development of the route would have maintained grain
prices in Siberia at a level satisfactory to producers.

The owners of the goldfields in Siberia were also inter-
ested in opening up the Northern Sea Route; it would have
been profitable for them to import foreign machinery for
the gold-mining industry by that route, as well as consumer
goods for their workers. Foreign groups, too, showed great
interest in the route because it could help them in pene-
trating the vast Siberian sales market.

There were also, however, influential people who opposed
the opening up of a sea route. The use of such an outlet ran
contrary to the interests of the landowner-grain exporters
in Russia's European part, and also to those of the industrial bourgeoisie in the central regions, who at that time
enjoyed a monopoly in the Siberian market. These circles
could count on government protection.

The conflict involved in the establishment of a sea route
to Siberia revolved mainly around the question of the duty-
free import into Siberia of foreign goods. The entrepreneurs
demanded that, in view of the risks connected with sailing
through the ice-bound Kara Sea, goods yielding high profits
should be imported duty-free. They agreed to undertake
navigation of the Kara Sea only if free ports were established at the outlets of the Ob and Yenisei. However, this
would have given wide access for foreign goods to the Siberian market and would have fundamentally violated the
traditional policy of favouring national industry. Obviously,
in such a situation Russia's industry would not have been
able to compete with foreign-made goods. This explains the
government's refusal to help in organising the export of
Siberian grain via the northern seas.

During certain periods permission was granted to import
a limited variety of foreign goods duty-free, but this did
not offer sufficient incentive to entrepreneurs to undertake
the risk of establishing a sea route.

On January 5, 1912 the Norwegian-owned Siberian
Steamship Manufacturing and Trading Company, Ltd. was
founded in Oslo with the purpose of organising regular commercial sailings through the Kara Sea to Siberia. The found-
ers of the company had far-reaching plans: they wanted
to conquer the vast Siberian market, to obtain concessions

for the development of large forest areas and mineral resources, and to acquire agricultural land. I. Lead, an enterprising businessman and the initiator of the whole venture, was elected managing director. With the opening of the navigational season in 1913, the vessels of the company began to sail across the Kara Sea. The company secured influential friends among prominent Russian civil servants and entrepreneurs; in 1914 Lead was introduced to the tsar, who conferred upon him the title of "hereditary honorary citizen". His dual citizenship gave him many advantages. The company was exerting pressure to obtain permission to import goods duty-free; early in 1915 permission was granted for the duration of the war. The tsarist edict of February 26, 1917 gave it the right to import goods duty-free for a term of six years (up to 1922) by way of the Siberian rivers. The Siberian market was thus opened to foreign interests at the expense of Russia's own industry.

However, navigation to the lower Ob and Yenisei rivers was irregular. Many ships did not reach their destination: some sank, others returned because they could not pass through the thick ice. For 14 years (out of the total of 43 years, from 1876, when sailing was begun, to 1919) there was virtually no commercial navigation in the Kara Sea. The total amount of cargo carried across the Kara Sea in both directions during the pre-revolutionary period was only 55,000 tons.

After 1905 the government began to regard the Kara Sea not only as a sea route to the outlets of the Ob and the Yenisei but also as a militarily and strategically important section of the Northern Sea Route.

Hydrographic research was necessary prior to organising regular sailings on the Northern Sea Route. Two ice-breakers, the *Taimyr* and *Vaigach*, were built for this purpose in 1909 at the Nevsky shipyard in St. Petersburg. From their homeport of Vladivostok they began to carry out hydrographic surveys in 1910. As a result, a number of islands were discovered, among them Severnaya Zemlya.

In 1914 an expedition set out from Vladivostok with the object of sailing along the Northern Sea Route to Arkhangelsk. On October 4, 1914 the vessels rounded Cape Chelyuskin, were caught fast in the ice and compelled to drift all winter. The *Taimyr* and *Vaigach* reached Arkhangelsk only on September 16, 1915, after overcoming the enormous dif-

ficulties involved in sailing through heavy ice in an unchart-
ed sea. Thus, the two ice-breakers succeeded in negotiating
the Northern Sea Route in two navigational seasons.

The result of this expedition led the tsarist government
to the conclusion that the Northern Sea Route could not be
used for commercial shipping.

At the same time it remained extremely difficult to convey
goods to north-eastern Russia: cargoes had to be carried
across the whole of Siberia by railway to Irkutsk, thence
to the upper reaches of the Lena by the so-called Lena routes,
from there along the Lena River to Yakutsk and then carried thousands of kilometres to small population centres
lost in the vastness of Siberia. Since the coastal regions
of the North-East were accessible by sea, a part of the cargoes for the Kolyma region passed through the port of Ayan
on the Sea of Okhotsk. However, Russian vessels visited
the coasts of Kamchatka, Chukotka and the Okhotsk coast
rarely and irregularly. No military protection was provided
for Russian waters in the Far East. Furthermore, as we
have noted above, foreign goods were imported into the
area duty-free. All these factors served to promote foreign
expansion in Russian waters.

Penetration by the Americans of the Chukotka Peninsula,
the Anadyr region and Kamchatka began as early as the
mid-19th century and intensified after the winding-up of the
Russian-American Company and the sale of Alaska to the
USA (1867).

In the wake of American whalers, the schooners of numerous American and, to a lesser extent, Japanese trading
firms visited Russian shores. Rich Chukchi living on the
coast acted as middlemen between the US merchants and
the inhabitants of the tundra. The Americans began to set
up warehouses on the coast, to which they delivered various
goods from the USA during the summer. In winter the
Chukchi took these goods to the tundra regions and brought
back valuable furs, mammoth bone, etc., in exchange.

Between 1869 and 1884 a total of 2,339 American whaling-
ships visited the northern part of the Pacific Ocean, cruising
for the most part near the Russian coast.

Fishing areas near the Kamchatka coast were controlled
by the Americans in the mid-fifties and by the Japanese in
the eighties. A Russian fishing industry in the Kamchatka
waters was organised only in the nineties; however, the

Russian entrepreneurs, possessing little capital, soon fell under the influence of Japanese companies.

The fear that it would lose north-eastern Siberia prompted the government to organise, and from 1900 to subsidise, regular voyages between Vladivostok, the ports of the Okhotsk and Bering Seas and the Komandorskiye (Commander) Islands. The dispatch, following the Russo-Japanese War (1904-1905), of vessels to the Far Eastern shores of Russia's northern seas and the hydrographic surveys carried out by the *Taimyr* and *Vaigach* served to hasten the organising of regular sailings to the mouth of the Kolyma River. These began in 1911.

The history of the period examined in this section shows that Russia under capitalism lacked the means for large-scale development of her vast northern regions or for investigation of their natural wealth.

The Soviet Period

Study and Development
of the North During the Period of Economic Rehabilitation

A new attitude was adopted towards the economic development of the country's northern territories shortly after the establishment of the new social system in Russia. Scientific and prospecting teams were already being sent to the North in 1918; but many of them had to interrupt their work as a result of the outbreak of the Civil War and the seizure of parts of European Russia, and later also of the Asiatic North, by the whiteguards and foreign interventionists. A Commission for the Study and Practical Utilisation of the Russian North was set up and was notably active. The Northern Scientific and Commercial Expedition of the Supreme Economic Council was founded in March 1920; it was charged with equipping expeditions and co-ordinating and planning all scientific research and work associated with expeditions to be carried out by different organisations in the northern regions. The fact that the greatest scientists and public figures of the new Russia were drawn into the study of the North shows the great importance that was attached to the subject. The President of the Academy of Sciences, A. P. Karpinsky, was elected chairman of the expedition's scientific council; Academician A. Y. Fersman became his deputy. On the council were Maxim Gorky, the famous writer; Y. M. Shokalsky, the chairman of the Russian Geographic Society; Professor L. S. Berg, N. M. Knipovich, V. G. Tan-Bogoraz, K. M. Deryugin and others; its secretary was V. L. Komarov, who later became an academician and President of the Academy of Sciences of the Soviet Union. The expedition began its work in 1920.

The Soviet North was also studied by the Polar Commission and by a Permanent Commission for the Study of Russia's Natural Productive Forces, which operated under the aegis of the Academy of Sciences. In addition, a number of other organisations sent expeditions to the North. The scale of scientific research conducted in the North increased with each year.

Prospecting carried out over many years under the direction of Academician A. Y. Fersman (1920-1940), led to the discovery of huge deposits of apatite-nepheline ores in the Khibiny and Lovozero tundra, of nickel ore in the Monchetundra and of the Kovdor and Olenegorsk iron ore deposits amongst others. The hydrological-ichthyological team headed by Professors N. M. Knipovich and G. A. Klyuge studied the reserves of fish in the Barents Sea. In 1920, geological work was begun in the Ukhta district while a geological survey of the north-eastern European part of the country commenced in 1921. Prospecting carried out by a party headed by Professor A. A. Chernov led to the discovery of the Pechora coalfields.

Among early measures taken in the study of the Soviet North was the programme of research into the Arctic Ocean, begun in 1920. On March 16, 1921, a decree was published concerning the establishment of the Floating Marine Research Institute (Plavmornin), which was to comprise biological, hydrological, meteorological, geological and mineralogical departments. The programme of the institute, which conducted its work on board the expedition vessel *Persei*, provided for the study of the seas, estuaries and islands in the Arctic Ocean. From then on the systematic study of the Arctic seas was steadily extended in scope. The Committee for the Northern Sea Route, organised in 1920 in Siberia, was given responsibility for establishing regular navigation of the Arctic seas to the outlets of the biggest Siberian rivers—the Ob, Yenisei, Lena and Kolyma, organising trade with foreign countries and also for studying the resources of the Siberian North.

The Northern Scientific and Commercial Expedition organised several interdepartmental conferences. As a result of the extension of its activities, it was renamed in 1925 and became known as the Institute for the Study of the North. Later, in 1930, it formed the basis of the All-Union Arctic Institute (now the Arctic and Antarctic Research Institute), which concerned itself with the study of the seas of the Arctic Ocean and the Central Polar Basin and, up to 1939, of the geology and mineral resources of the Arctic coast as well.

The initial ventures and plans of the Soviet Government which were directed towards the study and development of the North were highly successful. They are indissolubly linked with the name of V. I. Lenin, the founder and leader of the Soviet state. Archive documents dating back to the period from 1918 to 1923 show that Lenin and his closest associates gave much attention to the question of the development of the North even during the eventful years in which Soviet power was established. This can be seen from Lenin's decrees on the organisation of Plavmornin and the protection of the ichthyological resources of the northern seas, from the government decision on the organisation of the Kara expeditions to the sea outlets of the Siberian rivers, from Lenin's extensive correspondence with Professor Knipovich on the establishing of a fleet of fishing trawlers in the Barents Sea and many of his notes, from his meetings with Gubkin, at which they discussed the development of the Ukhta oilfields, and his interest in every initiative connected with the study and development of the northern resources.

Documents relating to those early days are characterised by the conscious aim of drawing the as yet untapped and practically unexplored natural wealth of the northern areas into the country's economic life. Clearly foreseeing the vast prospects industrialisation founded on advanced technology would open up, the leaders of the Soviet state fully realised the great role the northern regions were destined to play in the country's economy.

* * *

Exploitation of the known resources of the European North was facilitated by the region's greater accessibility and by the railways that were already in existence there.

Utilisation of its natural wealth, in particular of its forests, was possible as early as the period of economic rehabilitation.

In the initial stages of the development of the north-western regions a major part was played by the Transport and Industrial Development Group of the Murmansk Railway; the group proved to be a very successful means of organising development of the northern regions.

As a consequence of the devastation resulting from the First World War and the Civil War the Murmansk Railway, which had been hurriedly built in connection with the war effort and had been opened, while still unfinished, in 1916, fell into a state of complete disrepair. In 1923 the managerial division of the Murmansk Railway was transformed into a special group, with the object of raising the level of economic activity in areas within the railway's range of influence. Means towards this end were to include development of a fishing and a lumber industry, increasing the resident population and completing construction of the Murmansk Railway and of the port of Murmansk. The group was placed in control of a wooded area of 3,000,000 dessiatines.[1] The diagram on the opposite page shows the organisational structure of the group and the inter-relations between its branches. The aims, for whose realisation it had been established, were attained in a few years. The economic development of the Karelo-Murmansk region and the greater volume of traffic handled by the port of Murmansk, which linked the Soviet Union with world markets, increased the amount of freight carried by the Murmansk Railway. Having fulfilled its pioneering role, the special group of the Murmansk Railway was dissolved in 1927 and its separate branches were merged with appropriate boards.

The exhaustion before the Revolution of the forests of Central and South Russia made exploitation of the forest areas in the North essential.

Development of the forests was begun in two regions: 1) the Northern Dvina basin, in the mouth of which lies Arkhangelsk, which was rapidly becoming the principal centre for timber processing in the USSR, and a port handling foreign trade, and 2) in the Vychegda basin, an area bordering on the Northern and the Murmansk (Kirovsk) railways

[1] Dessiatine—Russian measure of area of 1.09254 ha.—*Ed.*

DIAGRAM SHOWING PRODUCTION LINKS BETWEEN
THE SUB-UNITS OF THE MURMANSK RAILWAY GROUP

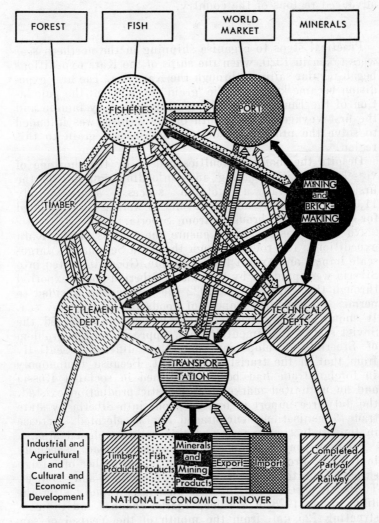

and the Onega River, in the mouth of which lies the port town of Onega. Timber-felling was also begun in the Pechora and Mezen river basins. The Karelian Autonomous Soviet Socialist Republic became an important timber-producing region. The European North became the principal source of timber both for export and for the central, economically advanced regions of the country.

* * *

Practical steps to organise shipping in the northern seas were taken in 1920, when the ships of the Kara expeditions began regular sailings through the Kara Sea. The first expedition became known as the "grain" expedition: the population of the European North was threatened by famine and the first voyage to the mouth of the Yenisei was intended to solve the problem of delivering Siberian grain to this region.

Despite the many difficulties caused by the shortage of vessels, fuel and loading and unloading equipment, the first voyage was a notable success: approximately 11,000 tons of grain and foodstuffs as well as furs intended for export were brought from Siberia.

No effort was spared to ensure the success of the Kara expeditions. The route through the Kara Sea made a large-scale import and export trade possible. Goods imported into Siberia were paid for by the sale of Siberian goods exported through the Kara Sea. In 1922 the government decided to permit the duty-free import of goods into Siberia by sea. It should be emphasised that this decision reflected the Soviet state's fundamentally new approach to the problem of Siberia's development, one that differed essentially from that of the tsarist government. Because a monopoly in foreign trade had been established in socialist Russia and an unlimited market for domestic production existed, the duty-free import of foreign goods into Siberia by state trade organisations encouraged an accelerated increase in the productive capacity of this underdeveloped area.

Siberian timber found a ready market abroad, especially in Britain. From 1924 on an increasing number of foreign ships began to visit the outlets of the Ob and Yenisei. Timber exports began to grow especially rapidly after the discovery in 1928 of the deep Igarka channel and the constructing 725 km. from the mouth of the Yenisei of saw mills and a harbour at Igarka. In contrast to the Ob, there are no bars at the mouth of the Yenisei, and large sea-going vessels can sail up the river as far as Igarka to take on cargo. Timber felled in the pine forests of the Angara valley, which is of a particularly high quality, was floated down to Igarka, dressed and exported.

In addition to developing marine transport and shipping on the Ob and Yenisei rivers, the Committee for the Northern Sea Route carried on studies of the natural wealth of Siberia's North. In 1921 it discovered the copper-nickel ore deposits near Norilsk, graphite on the Nizhnyaya Tunguska, etc.

In the Far East, ships of the regular Arctic expeditions began to call again at ports on the north-east Siberian coast. The Kamchatka joint-stock company (AKO) was organised in 1921 and placed under the control of the People's Commissariat for Foreign Trade; it was charged with the development of deep-sea fishing, the investigation of Kamchatka's natural wealth and with the expansion of the region's economy. Subsequently a large fishing industry was created on Kamchatka and other branches of economic activity encouraged.

Economic Development
of the North During the Period of Industrialisation

The revival of the national economy was accompanied by its restructuring. When the pre-war level of industrial production was reached in 1928, a massive industrialisation drive was launched. Industry was expanded in the old centres of production while being introduced into fresh areas. In the relocation of productive capacity the accent was placed on the development of the eastern territories, with their vast natural resources. Thus, in a short time the Urals became a leading area in the production of steel and other metals; new coal- and ore-mining regions were opened up in Western Siberia and Kazakhstan; and industrial development of vast areas of Central Asia and the Transcaucasia was begun.

Study and development of the economic potential of the northern territories were intensified during the industrialisation period. Many valuable natural resources were discovered there which were not to be found or were obtainable only in negligible quantities elsewhere in the USSR. Some of these resources were of unique quality.

The European North developed with especial rapidity. Timber-felling increased annually; saw mills, pulp-and-

27

MAIN INDUSTRIAL CENTRES IN RUSSIA'S EUROPEAN NORTH IN 1913 (WITHIN THE SOVIET UNION'S PRESENT BOUNDARIES)

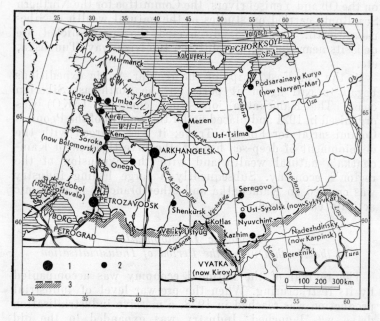

Industrial centres:
1. medium
2. small

3. Southern boundary of the North

paper mills and plants to extract chemicals from timber were built. Exploitation of the forests of Karelia and the Northern Dvina, Pechora and Mezen basins was begun. A greater proportion of timber produced in the European North, practically all of which had been exported before the Revolution, began to reach building sites in the European part of the USSR.

The Khibiny apatites on the Kola Peninsula (Murmansk Region) discovered by the early expeditions of Fersman, which were now being mined, became the basic raw material for the production of phosphate fertilisers; mining of the copper-nickel ores in the Monchetundra was started, while

MAIN INDUSTRIAL CENTRES IN THE EUROPEAN
NORTH OF THE USSR

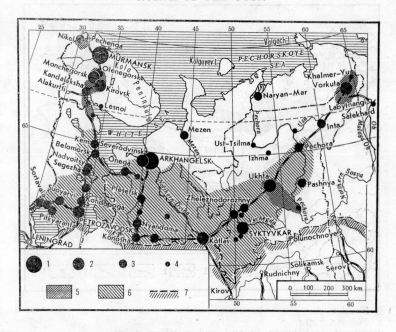

Industrial centres:
1. very big
2. big
3. medium
4. small

5. Intensive development of mineral resources
6. Intensive development of timber resources
7. Southern boundary of the North

extraction of the deposits in the Petsamo region commenced
after the Second World War. As a result Murmansk Region
became a major centre of the non-ferrous metal industry.
The iron ore deposits in Murmansk Region supplied ore to
the Cherepovets iron and steel works. Murmansk became
the principal operations centre for the trawler fleet and
fishing industry in the Soviet Union. The Kondopoga and
Segezha pulp-and-paper combines commenced activity in
Karelia. Machinery for the timber industry was also manufactured. Arkhangelsk became the major centre of the timber

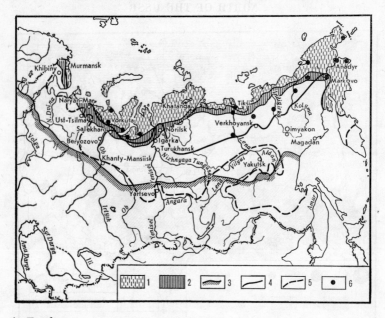

1. Tundra
2. Forest-tundra
3. Boundary between central and southern taiga
4. Present northern boundary of agricultural zone (vegetable-growing on open ground)
5. Northern boundary of agricultural zone in 1926 (acc. to Prof. I. F. Makarov)
6. "Oases" of greens and early vegetable-growing on open ground

industry in the Soviet Union and an important port in the European North. The economically important Belomorsk-Obozerskaya railway, linking Arkhangelsk Region with the Karelian Autonomous Soviet Socialist Republic and Murmansk Region, was built during the Second World War.

Exploitation of oil and natural gas deposits discovered in the Ukhta district was started in 1930. In the post-war period the rich Timano-Pechora oil- and gas-bearing province was discovered in the Komi Autonomous Soviet Socialist Republic.

Within the Pechora coalfield the Vorkuta deposits were the first to be developed. Prospecting in the region and its initial exploitation (in the 1930s) were rendered extremely difficult as a result of remoteness and lack of transport. In 1942 the 1,200-kilometre-long Pechora Railway, linking Kotlas and Vorkuta, began operation. The Konosha-Velsk-Kotlas railway, built a few years later, provided the shortest outlet for coal mined in Pechora coalfield to Leningrad and Arkhangelsk Region. River transport expanded on all navigable rivers, in particular on the Northern Dvina, Vychegda and Pechora. New ports were constructed on the White Sea and the Murmansk coast.

Thus, the years of socialist construction were characterised in the European North by massive industrialisation. This in turn necessitated an increase in the area of land under cultivation in the northern regions. "Agricultural oases" had long been farmed in the southern parts of Karelia, Arkhangelsk Region and the Komi ASSR and stock-breeding was also pursued in these areas. Among its other functions, the already mentioned Murmansk Railway Group succeeded in extending agricultural activity northwards. The Khibiny experimental agricultural centre on the Kola Peninsula was opened in 1923. Experimental work was carried on there for many years by the agronomist I. G. Eichfeld, the pioneer of polar agriculture in the USSR (at present member of the All-Union Lenin Academy of Agricultural Sciences). The pioneers of polar agriculture carried out extensive research and experimental work, as a result of which they succeeded in developing strains of vegetables resistant to the low temperatures of the North in addition to other high-yield crops. Seeds were sent from Khibiny to all areas of the North where experimental plots had been established. As a result, agriculture in the Far North became possible.

* * *

In order to intensify exploitation of the resources of northern Siberia and, in particular, to organise the export of timber and other commodities through the Kara Sea, the Committee for the Northern Sea Route was reorganised in 1928 into the North Siberian State Joint-Stock Company for Trade and Industry. This regional transport-industrial organisation, similar to the special group of the Murmansk Railway, assumed control of the economy of a vast area—the Ob and Yenisei regions.

The company initiated a wide range of activities. Timber-felling along the banks of the Angara was organised, logs were floated down the Yenisei for processing in Igarka and export; in the Ob basin the cutting of timber for export through Ob Guba (Inlet) was begun. The company controlled all commercial navigation on the Ob and Yenisei rivers and the Kara Sea as well as all ice patrols and passenger air traffic between Krasnoyarsk and Igarka and between Omsk and the mouth of the Ob. As a result of its efforts powerful diesel-engined ships (up to 1,500 h. p.), steel and wooden lighters and many other vessels began to appear on the Ob and Yenisei rivers. It also carried out pioneering work in the exploitation of the mineral wealth of the Yenisei area: the mining of graphite was initiated on the Kureika and Nizhnyaya Tunguska, and extraction was started of large deposits of coal, fire-clay and other minerals. Fishing, hunting and trapping were organised along the lower reaches of the Ob and Yenisei, in Yenisei Bay and Ob Guba while experimental work was pursued in Yartsevo, Igarka and other areas in order to further the development of agriculture in the North. Several associated industrial centres with a common transport system and under a joint management fell within the organisational structure of the company.

The systematic study of the Arctic seas, expeditions to the Far North and the accumulation of experience relating to the sea routes across the Kara Sea to Siberia and across the Chukotka Sea to the outlets of the Kolyma were pre-requisites for the organisation of direct sailings on the Northern Sea Route.

In December 1932, following the epoch-making voyage of the ice-breaker *Sibiryakov*, which traversed the Northern Sea Route in a single navigational season, the Principal Directorate for the Northern Sea Route was set up.

To establish normal commercial sailings along the ice-bound sea route on a firm basis a comprehensive programme was worked out that provided, amongst other things, for the building of ice-breakers, the construction of ports and coal-supply depots along the Northern Sea Route, the organising of ice patrols and freight transport by aircraft, the intensification of research work, the building of polar stations and the study of the Arctic seas.

The Principal Directorate for the Northern Sea Route

(Glavsevmorput) was a pioneer organisation whose aim was to develop the economy of the regions bordering on the Arctic seas. It subsumed all the activities of the North Siberian State Joint-Stock Company and its range of responsibility was extended in 1934 to include the islands and seas of the Arctic Ocean in the European part of the USSR and the entire land-mass north of the 62° N. (the line of latitude running through the town of Yakutsk) in the Asiatic part. All enterprises of national importance in this area were placed under its control, in particular those directed by the North Siberian State Joint-Stock Company, which ceased to exist as an independent entity. Glavsevmorput was also given responsibility for the economic and cultural welfare of the population of the North, which included the conducting of trade and the procurement of goods.

Glavsevmorput became a major organisation, in charge of a huge area and characterised by multifarious activities in the fields of transport, industry, trade and science.

Later, when navigation in the ice-bound Arctic seas had become commonplace, Glavsevmorput was dissolved; at present all shipping on the Northern Sea Route is under the control of the Ministry of Merchant Marine.

The history of Arctic exploration and the organisation of regular navigation of the Arctic seas is a record of daring and self-sacrifice. Dozens of polar research stations were built on the islands and shores of the Arctic seas to pursue comprehensive hydrographic and hydrological research, to mark the sea route by means of navigation signs and to carry out special expeditions to high northern latitudes. A notable event was the landing on the North Pole in the summer of 1937 of an expedition led by O. Y. Schmidt; in the course of the expedition the station North Pole-1, under the command of I. D. Papanin, was set up, which reached the shores of Greenland on a drifting ice-floe. Drifting stations have since become the standard method of studying the Arctic seas.

The dispatching by the Northern Sea Route to the Lena River of two powerful motorships established a necessary basis for navigation of the lower reaches of that river. River vessels began to appear on the Yana and Kolyma rivers and in the mouth of the Khatanga River. The rivers became extensions of the Northern Sea Route into the very heart of the northern area, thus broadening the range of influence of Glavsevmorput to cover the vast territory of the Asiatic North.

The legendary exploit of the *Chelyuskin* expedition marked the beginning of the development of air transport in the Asiatic North. In 1934 O. Y. Schmidt attempted a direct sailing along the Northern Sea Route in the merchant ship *Chelyuskin*. The vessel became stuck in the ice near the Bering Strait and sank after a long period of drifting. Over a hundred people landed on an ice-floe and Soviet planes were sent to transfer the entire expedition from the ice to the mainland. The rescue directly stimulated the development of air transport in the Asiatic part of the Arctic. Air routes and support bases were established and regular flights as far as Tiksi Bay were organised; long non-stop flights were made and thus a network of air routes covering the Arctic came into existence. Airplanes were also extensively used for ice patrols.

In 1923 large gold deposits were discovered on the Aldan. The building of the Amur-Yakutsk motor road, which ran for 728 km. from the Bolshoi Never station on the Amur Railway to Tommota, was completed in 1930; after the war it was continued to Yakutsk. The building of the road accelerated the study and development of the huge Aldan mining and industrial area. In addition to gold, phlogopitemica was mined there; in the fifties the big Chulman coalfield and the Aldan iron ore province were discovered.

The new motor road leading from Zayarsk, on the Angara River, to Ust-Kut, where the navigable section of the Lena begins, was completed in 1932. This road linked the two routes by which goods were brought into Yakutia: from the north, by sea through the port of Tiksi; and from the south, through Ust-Kut. However, the limited bearing capacity of the road and the high cost of freight haulage checked the development of industry in the Yakut ASSR. The building after the war of the Taishet-Ust-Kut railway, which came into operation in 1950, was aimed at removing this obstacle.

The railway radically altered the transport situation in Yakutia and the northern Irkutsk region. It lowered the cost per ton of transporting freight to the navigable section of the Lena River by 80-90 per cent. The volume of goods brought into the Yakut ASSR soon multiplied several times.

The development of systems of sea, river and air routes

MAIN INDUSTRIAL CENTRES IN RUSSIA'S ASIATIC NORTH IN 1913
(WITHIN THE SOVIET UNION'S PRESENT BOUNDARIES)

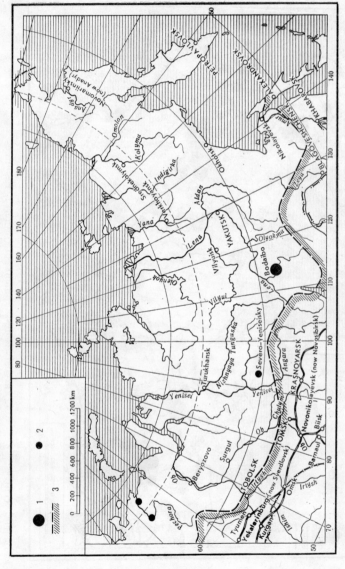

Industrial centres:

1. medium 2. small 3. Southern boundary of the North

3*

MAIN INDUSTRIAL CENTRES IN THE ASIATIC NORTH OF THE USSR

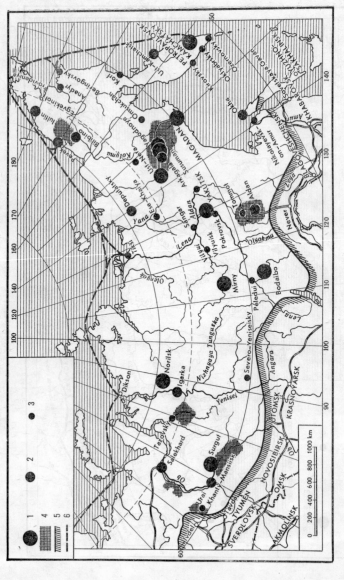

Industrial centres:

1. big
2. medium
3. small

4. Intensive development of mineral resources
5. Southern boundary of the North
6. Northern Sea Route

in the Arctic facilitated the expansion of prospecting activity in the north-east of the country; it was also a factor contributing towards the exploitation of a variety of mineral deposits. Prospecting for oil and salt was begun in the thirties in Nordvik and Kozhevnikovo bays and resulted in the discovery of deposits of commercial significance. However, remoteness and inaccessibility hindered their exploitation. The Sangar-Khaiya coalfields on the Lena, which became the main source of fuel of the Yakut ASSR, were brought into production; coal from these deposits was also used by vessels while crossing the central section of the Northern Sea Route. Large tin deposits were discovered on the Yana River; high-grade coal was found on the Zyryanka, a tributary of the Kolyma.

The first geological expeditions in 1928 and 1930 had discovered potentially highly productive goldfields along the upper reaches of the Kolyma, whose exploitation was now begun. Later, large deposits of gold were also discovered along the upper reaches of the Indigirka River, while tin was found in the Chukotka Peninsula. Development was begun of the huge area which now forms Magadan Region and north-eastern Yakutia. Motor roads were built to link various regions with the Kolyma trunk road; many seaports, including Nagayevo, Egvekinot and Pevek were also constructed.

The area adjoining the upper reaches of the Kolyma and Indigirka became the leading centre of the Soviet Union's gold and tin industry. After the war development was begun of a new centre for the gold industry on Chaunskaya Guba, in the Bolshaya and Malaya Anyui river basins. It focussed on the town of Bilibino.

Utilisation of Kamchatka's natural resources was also begun; its southern part reached a high level of economic development while a number of fish-processing plants were established on its western and eastern coasts. Kamchatka Region became one of the main centres of the fishing industry in the USSR.

The extraction of oil and gas was initiated in the northern part of Sakhalin Island, which became a major source of fuel for the southern part of the Soviet Far East.

However, the great advances achieved in the study and development of the natural resources of the Soviet North during the past 50 years are only a beginning.

CHAPTER TWO
THE NORTH IN THE SOVIET ECONOMY

1. Natural Conditions and Development

Definition of "the Soviet North". The term "Soviet North" was already widespread within a few years after the establishment of Soviet power. In the twenties various collections of articles dealing with the problems of the North bore the general designation, "The Soviet North"; later, a monthly journal was published under this title.

The boundaries of the areas included in the Soviet North were not strictly demarcated and different authors applied the name to different regions. The first attempt to define the southern boundaries of the Soviet North, in the economic sense, was made by the present author in *The Distribution of the Productive Forces in the North During the Second Five-Year Period*, published in 1933.

A study of the development of industry and transport in the northern regions over a long period of time enables us to establish criteria by which the borders of the North can be defined with a higher degree of accuracy than was previously possible. These criteria are as follows:

1. Location to the north of the long-settled and economically developed areas of the country and remoteness from the big industrial centres from which development of the natural resources of the northern regions could be initiated.

2. Harsh natural conditions, inimical to the expansion of agricultural activity, which also made general development of the area more difficult as a result of long and cold winters, widespread permafrost, marshiness, etc.

3. Extremely low population density and a less developed industrial base, transport network and general economy in comparison with long-settled areas.

4. A greater expenditure of man-hours in the exploitation of natural resources than would be required for the exploitation of similar resources in areas lying further south.

If the above criteria are employed, the following areas should be regarded as comprising the Soviet North: in European USSR, Murmansk and Arkhangelsk regions and the Karelian and Komi ASSRs; in Asiatic USSR, the Yamalo-Nenets and Khanty-Mansi national areas of Tyumen Region, the northern districts of Tomsk Region, the Taimyr and Evenk national areas, the Turukhansk and Igarka districts of Krasnoyarsk Territory; the Yakut ASSR, Magadan and Kamchatka regions, the northern districts of Irkutsk, Chita, Amur and Sakhalin regions, the Buryat ASSR and Khabarovsk Territory (see map on p. 40).

A study of knowledge gained from the development of the North reveals essential differences in the nature and degree of the development of its constituent regions, differences directly stemming from the geographical position of each region in relation to centres from which development could be initiated, mass markets and national railway systems. In those northern regions which possess rail links with the country's railway network and also in regions located in the vicinity of big industrial centres, factors tending to raise costs exert a much smaller influence than they do in regions remote from development centres and the markets which absorb the output of the North. In regions falling into the first category population density is many times higher than in the second.

Thus, it seems correct to divide the northern territory into two sub-zones: the Near and the Far North.

We have included in the Far North the tundra and forest-tundra zones, and also in part the taiga, which is in general far removed from the railway network and located in the higher latitudes, where severe natural conditions make acclimatisation difficult. The factors tending to raise costs, of which we shall speak at greater length in Chapter Three, are particularly significant here. Any kind of work carried out in these areas costs from 1.5 to 3 times as much as it would if undertaken in the regions lying to the south of the northern zone.

The Near North includes areas which enjoy more favourable natural conditions and are located relatively closer to the railway network and the big industrial centres. Conditions here favour the establishment of a more developed industrial structure than in the Far North, while at the same time a certain amount of agriculture (stock-breeding,

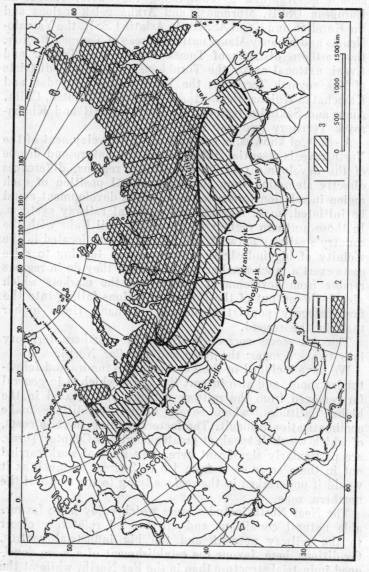

THE SOVIET NORTH

1. Southern boundary of the North 2. Far North 3. Near North.

vegetable- and potato-growing) is possible. Those factors which tend to raise costs have a much weaker impact in the Near North; given the existence of railways, costs multiply by no more than 1.5 times.

Thus, the relative proximity of the European North to the economically developed parts of the country (the central and western regions) and its rail connections with them have promoted its more rapid development and made it possible to utilise on a considerable scale its timber, coal, apatites and iron ore. Consequently, as we have already noted, the productive forces in the European North of the Soviet Union have, in general, grown considerably. Conversely, the remoteness of the Asiatic North from the economically developed regions of the country has checked its development.

The Near North has a tendency to expand. However, even in the distant future there will still exist vast areas in the North with a very severe climate, where the conditions of life will always be harder and where factors raising costs will always be more potent than in other parts of the country. Even after the building of a railway network these areas will still have to be seen in relation to the Far North. These are the regions north of the Arctic Circle in the European USSR, the northern regions of Western and Eastern Siberia, the Ob and the Yenisei North, the northern part of Yakutia, Magadan Region, the northern part of the coast of the Sea of Okhotsk and of Kamchatka Region up to approximately 60° N, embracing an area of about 5,000,000 sq. km., or almost 25 per cent of the total area of the USSR.

Let us examine some of the features specific to the Soviet North.

Climate. In evaluating the region from the viewpoint of its suitability for agriculture, the principal factors to be taken into account are atmospheric temperature, the type of soil cover, the duration of the frost-free period, and the intensity and duration of insolation (solar radiation). The most important factor to be considered when examining problems linked with the conditions required for acclimatisation, the utilisation of machinery and the development of industry is the degree of climatic severity, which is determined by a combination of elements, including temperature and wind velocity, humidity and various biological factors.

In the European North climatic conditions are not as

41

severe as they are in the Asiatic zone but here too the climate and the soils are little suited to agriculture. Podzolic soils, some of which may be cultivated, are found only in its southern districts. Most of the region has peat-bog and peat-podzolic gley soils of a mechanically coarse composition, in addition to rocks and rocky soils. The mean temperature in January, in areas of the European North such as Naryan-Mar, Ust-Vorkuta, Ust-Ukhta, is 17-20°C below zero, while the mean temperature in July is plus 12.2-15.7°C; the mean annual temperatures in the North range from minus 1.4° to minus 6.3°C. The number of frost-free days is 33-50 per cent lower in the North than it is in relatively nearby areas which are not included in the northern zone (Leningrad, Cherepovets, Vologda, Perm, etc.).

Murmansk, on the coast of the ice-free Barents Sea, and Petrozavodsk and Syktyvkar, in southern Karelia and Komi respectively, have higher mean annual air temperatures, although the number of frost-free days is small, and light frosts can occur during the summer. The eastern and north-eastern areas of the European North have the most severe climate, with sub-zero mean annual temperatures, few frost-free days, strong winds and sharp temperature fluctuations between day- and night-time in most places.

The climate in North Siberia is even harsher. Typical of the entire territory of the North of the Asiatic part of the USSR are mean annual sub-zero temperatures, ranging from minus 4 and minus 6.7°C in Beryozovo and Salekhard (on the Ob) to minus 10.7°C and minus 11.9°C in Dudinka and Seimchan. The mean January temperatures are minus 22.4°C in Beryozovo, minus 24.4°C in Salekhard, minus 29.6°C in Igarka and 39.5°C in Seimchan. At times the temperature drops to 60°C below zero. In Seimchan there are only 55 frost-free days a year. Compact or insular permafrost is found practically throughout the Asiatic North. The low-lying areas are marshy.

On the whole the climatic conditions here do not favour agriculture. Only in a few areas, between the Lena and the Aldan rivers in Yakutia, for example, is crop farming possible, and even there the labour expenditure per unit of production is several times higher than in Siberia's southern agricultural regions.

The maps on pages 40 and 44 give a general idea of the

basic climatic features of the North. On the basis of a comprehensive study of climatic factors conducted by V. F. Burkhanov it is possible to distinguish four zones with climates of varying degrees of severity.

The first zone, the one with the harshest climate, embraces the tundra of the Asiatic part of the USSR. The climate is also extremely severe in the second and most of the third zone, including Murmansk Region, northern districts of Karelia, Arkhangelsk Region and the Komi Autonomous Republic, large areas of the Yamalo-Nenets and Khanty-Mansi national areas, southern Taimyr and northern Evenk national areas, Yakutia except its southernmost areas, Magadan and Kamchatka regions and the Okhotsk and Ayano-Maisky districts of Khabarovsk Territory.

Acclimatisation is most difficult in the first and second zones, especially for people from the southern parts of the country. It is somewhat easier to acclimatise in the southern parts of the third zone.

Typical of all three zones is the almost universal spread of permafrost (except in the western part of the third zone) and extreme bogginess. Machinery designed for more moderate climates often breaks down. Machines of "Arctic design", made of frost-resistant metals and materials, have to be used in these parts. Cross-country vehicles with a crawler drive are the main means of transport in use apart from the railways.

In the first and second zones it is extremely difficult to develop agriculture. In the third zone vegetables and even grain crops can be grown in a few places.

The fourth zone extends largely beyond the North proper. The climate here is relatively favourable for human life and agricultural activity.

Natural resources. The study of the Soviet North is still very incomplete. A general geological survey has been made for the purpose of establishing the existence of mineral deposits there. The search for economic minerals is limited to the most promising districts, which are to be given priority in development. However, even the relatively superficial studies made so far show that the North possesses great mineral wealth, representing a considerable part of the Soviet Union's known reserves. These deposits are concentrated in relatively small areas and have a higher ore content than in other parts of the country. These two factors make it

CLIMATIC SEVERITY ZONES (ACC. TO V. F. BURKHANOV)

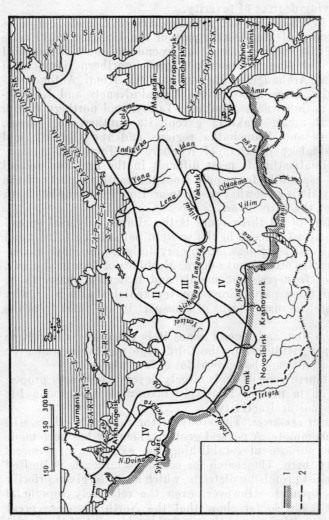

Zone I—mean yearly severity—3.5–4.6 Burkhanov points
Zone II—   ,,   ,,   —2.5–3.5   ,,   ,,
Zone III—   ,,   ,,   —2.5–2.2   ,,   ,,
Zone IV—   ,,   ,,   —1.6–2.2   ,,   ,,

1. Southern border of the North 2. Southern border of Sub-zone IV

worthwhile exploiting them despite all the difficulties involved.

The northern territories contain over 60 per cent of the country's known natural gas reserves and over two-fifths of the known oil reserves. Most of these reserves are concentrated in two areas—the West Siberian and the Timano-Pechora (Komi ASSR), with a total area of oil and gas deposits exceeding 1,500,000 sq. km. and 600,000 sq. km. respectively. A big concentration of gas, accounting for about one-fifth of the country's known reserves, has been discovered in the Lena-Vilyui oil-bearing area in Yakutia.

A profusion of non-ferrous and noble metals, rare elements and valuable minerals is found in the North. Most of the known reserves of nickel and titanium, a large part of the gold, tin and bauxite reserves, virtually all the diamond reserves, and the apatite-nepheline ore deposit (the only one in the USSR and largest in the world), a large part of the rare elements, found in special deposits and also as components of the ores of other raw materials, most amber mica and the main Muscovite mica reserves are all concentrated in that part of the USSR. About 50 per cent of the Soviet Union's commercial timber grows in the North. There are also big coalfields—the Pechora, Tunguska, Lena, Chulman and others—estimated to contain the larger part of the geological coal reserves of the USSR.

We have only pointed out the groups of minerals of the northern zone which are particularly important to the development of modern industry. Naturally, there are also many other minerals (iron, mineral building materials, etc.), the transportation of which to other parts of the country is not going to be economically expedient in the foreseeable future.

Forests occupy large areas in the North; the density of forests is much higher in the northern territories than it is in the more southern ones, where the timber reserves have been exhausted to a considerable degree. Timber-felling is concentrated in districts lying close to rivers along which the timber can be floated to the nearest railway.

There are certain areas of the North where various valuable natural resources are particularly abundant. Among them are the Kola Peninsula, the Ukhta district of the Komi ASSR, the Ob North, Norilsk Region, a number of north-eastern territories (Western Yakutia, Chukotka and others). Naturally, the co-ordinated development of such areas makes it possible to use these resources most effectively. In that case the expenditure connected with the setting up of the infrastructure—the building of roads, power stations, towns, workers' settlements, etc.—is relatively smaller than it would be if only some of the resources in different districts were developed.

Population. In pre-Soviet times the northern territories were very sparsely populated. In the European North the population consisted of Russians and the relatively small Komi people; in the Asiatic North, where the share of Russians was very small, the indigenous population consisted of the Yakuts (a little over than 200,000), the Nentsi, Evenks, Khanty, Mansi, Nganasans, Selkups, Dolgans, Yukagirs, Chukchi, Eskimos, Koryaks, Itelmens, Kets, Evens, Nivkhis, Orochi, Oroki, Aleuts, Saami, Ents and others. Part of them also lived in the European North.

A substantial population influx began only in the twenties of this century in connection with the economic development of the natural resources of the North.

These migrants (either to settle permanently or work on contracts for a limited period—miners, builders, engineers and so on) mainly went to live in existing or newly built towns and settlements. As a result, the North is highly urbanised—more so even than the most industrial areas of the Soviet Union. In our first and second zones there is a great preponderance of males, as is generally the case in developing areas, since men of an able-bodied age tend to first arrive without their families.

The average population density is very low—0.6 per 1 sq. km. It is highest in the European North, with 3 per sq. km., but even here the population is concentrated mainly in areas close to railways, rivers, and also, to a lesser degree, the coast. Elsewhere, vast tracts are practically uninhabited. Thus, the Nenets National Area, in the tundra zone, has a density of only 0.2 per 1 sq. km.

The table below shows the population density and distribution in the European North as compared with the regions to the south.

The figures show a sharp difference in population density between the European North and the contiguous areas to the south. They also show the high proportion of urban

Population of the European North of the USSR

	Area in thousands of sq. km.	Population in thousands according to January 1970 census		Percentage urban	Density of population, persons per sq. km.
		Total	Urban		
Northern areas					
Karelian ASSR	172.4	714	491	69	4.1
Komi ASSR	415.9	965	598	62	2.3
Murmansk Region	144.9	799	708	89	5.5
Arkhangelsk Region including	587.4	1,402	921	66	2.4 (3.3)[1]
Nenets National Area	176.7	39	21	55	0.2
Total for European North	1,320.6	3,880	2,718	70	2.9
Contiguous areas to the south					
Vologda Region	145.7	1,296	616	48	9.0
Leningrad Region	85.9	5,386	4,821	90 (61)[2]	62.7 (16.7)[2]
Perm Region	160.6	3,024	2,031	67	18.9

[1] Excluding Nenets National Area
[2] Excluding Leningrad

dwellers in the North. Thus, in Murmansk Region the percentage is 89, which is almost as high as in the highly industrialised Leningrad Region (including Leningrad, the second city with over 3 mln. inhabitants), while in the Nenets National Area it is higher than in the relatively developed Vologda Region.

Most of the inhabitants are permanent residents, and their descendants of the second and third generation are now the "natives" of the region. Even though the economy is steadily advancing, less and less people are being hired in other regions and there is only a shortage of skilled personnel. The southern parts of Arkhangelsk Region and the Karelian and Komi ASSRs have a large rural population.

The present population of the Asiatic North can be seen from the following table:

Population of the Asiatic North

	Area in thousands of sq. km.	Population in thousands according to January 1970 census		Percentage urban	Density of population, persons per sq. km.
		Total	Urban		
North of Western Siberia including national areas of Tyumen Region:	1,513.4	561	283	51	0.4
Khanty-Mansi	523.1	272	171	63	0.5
Yamalo-Nenets	750.3	80	34	43	0.1
North of Eastern Siberia including national areas of Krasnoyarsk Territory:	1,629.7	187	164	88	0.1
Evenk	767.6	13	4	28	0.02
Taimyr (Dolgano-Nenets) including the town of Norilsk[1]	862.1	174	160	92	0.2
ditto, without Norilsk	862.1	38	24	62	0.04
North-East of the USSR including:	4,811.8	1,378	944	69	0.3
Yakut ASSR	3,103.2	664	375	56	0.2
Magadan Region including:	1,199.1	352	263	75	0.3
Chukotka National Area	737.7	101	70	69	0.1
Kamchatka Region	472.3	287	219	76	0.6
including: Koryak National Area	301.5	31	11	34	0.1
Total for the Asiatic North	7,954.9	2,126	1,391	66	0.2
Contiguous areas to the south					
Novosibirsk Region	178.2	2,505	1,638	65	14.1
Southern part of Tyumen Region	162.0	1,055	485	46	6.5
Southern part of Tomsk Region	76.9	576	394	68	7.5
Southern part of Krasnoyarsk Territory	771.9	2,775	1,667	60	3.5
Southern part of Amur Region	148.0	718	449	62	4.8
Southern part of Khabarovsk Territory	329.6	1,187	1,002	84	3.6

[1] Norilsk, 136,000.

In the regions of the Asiatic North where industrial centres have been established, the proportion of urban dwellers is even higher than in the European North. Thus, it is as much as 92 per cent in the Taimyr National Area, 75 per cent in Magadan Region and 76 per cent in Kamchatka Region. This is because agriculture has been developing in the southern part of the European North long since, even though on a limited scale, whereas in the Asiatic North, except Central Yakutia, there was no agriculture at all.

The contrast in density between the northern areas and adjacent areas to the south in Asiatic USSR is especially sharp in the case of Tyumen Region and Krasnoyarsk Territory, where the density in the northern part is only a fraction of that in the southern part. This applies to the rest of Eastern Siberia and the Far East, although even in the southern districts the density is much lower than in the areas of traditional settlement in European USSR.

Typical of the Asiatic North is that few of the many newcomers "acclimatise" and settle for good. Thus, in Magadan Region, where the mechanical increase is 90 per cent of the total increase, 25-28 per cent of the population is renewed yearly. But here, too, the settled population is on the increase.

The proportion of people of employable age is high among the urban population. In Magadan Region they account for more than 90 per cent. The most numerous age group is that of people between the ages of 20 and 39.

Even though the proportion of urban dwellers is very high in the North, there are relatively few towns there, and only two of them—Arkhangelsk and Murmansk—have a population of over 250,000. Together they account for over 25 per cent of the total urban population of the European North. In the Asiatic North there are no such big towns, but three towns with a population of between 80,000 and 130,000 (Magadan, Yakutsk, Norilsk) account for over one-sixth of the total urban population. Most towns have a population below 20,000. The small number of towns in the North is compensated by hundreds of urban-type settlements, in which the bulk of the population resides.

Industry. The North accounts for only 3 per cent of the Soviet Union's total industrial output, which would hardly seem to represent a more than marginal importance in the Soviet economy. In actual fact, however, this figure is somewhat misleading, since the northern regions play a major, and in some cases dominant, role in the production of certain industrial items essential to the country's economic advance. They account for almost the total production of diamonds, most of the nickel, four-fifths of the phosphate raw material, a large part of the gold, tin, tungsten, mica, more than a third of the timber, one-fifth of the paper, one-third of the total catch of fish, a large part of the fur, etc. The North supplies a large share of the export commodities and justifies being called the country's "foreign currency mint".

As will be shown in greater detail in the next chapter, the difficulties connected with the development of the northern regions and the great increase in the cost of all the work carried out there make it necessary to adopt a selective approach to the development of the resources of the North, only those highly effective economically being utilised.

A set of enterprises has been set up in the North to secure the normal functioning of the leading industries and provide favourable living conditions for the population. That is why manufacturing is being developed alongside the extractive industries. In particular, repair workshops and engineering works are being set up in many districts to satisfy the requirements of the basic branches of production (ship repair and ship-building, the building of machinery for the timber and timber-processing industry, etc.).

Agriculture and Traditional Occupations. The development of agriculture in the northern regions is of great importance in creating normal living conditions for the local population and for people arriving from other parts of the country. That is why the growing of agricultural produce for local consumption is an important aspect of economic development there.

However, because of unfavourable natural conditions, agriculture is poorly developed and confined mainly to stock-breeding and vegetable-growing. Over 50 per cent of the total sown area (about 600,000 hectares according to 1968 data) is in the European North, where the natural conditions are more favourable than in the Asiatic North, and especially in the southern districts of Arkhangelsk

Region, the Komi ASSR and Karelia. The European North also accounts for over two-thirds of all the fodder crops and potatoes grown in the North. In many districts of the North vegetable and potato yields equal those obtained in zones with a moderate climate.

At the beginning of 1969 there were about 1,000,000 head of cattle. Roughly half were concentrated in the European North, where dairy and meat cattle has been bred for a very long time. Raised in the northern climate, the Kholmogory breed of cows, which gives high milk yields and has acclimatised very well, has won wide acclaim. In the Asiatic North cattle is bred mainly in Yakutia and northern Tomsk Region. Droving horse-breeding is widespread in Yakutia.

The labour expenditure on agricultural produce and the remuneration of labour are much higher in the northern districts than they are in the districts to the south. The cost of the output is from 1.5 to 3 times as high as it is in more favourable natural conditions, and in some regions of the Far North as much as 5-6 times.

Reindeer-breeding, hunting and fishing are traditional occupations. The USSR has the biggest reindeer herds (2,500,000 head) in the world, providing food and hides. Fish and reindeer meat supplement the diet of the population in the towns and settlements of the North.

Russian furs are world-renowned and the fur procured in the North is an important export item. In recent decades fur-farming has spread rapidly. Many fur farms breed silver and polar foxes, mink of various colour and other fur-bearing animals. Reindeer-breeding waste, the meat of sea mammals and fish are used to feed the animals. Part of the feed is brought from other districts. Where local feed is used, fur-farming is very profitable.

The map on pages 52-53 gives a general idea about the specialisation of agriculture and traditional occupations in the North.

Transport. In the North the building of the transport network was linked mainly with the development of natural resources. Thus, the opening up of the Pechora coalfields led to the building of the Pechora Railway (Kotlas-Vorkuta), the exploitation of the gold and mica fields in Southern Yakutia to that of the Amur-Yakutia motor road, later continued to the town of Yakutsk, and the Kolyma motor road was built when the goldfields along the upper

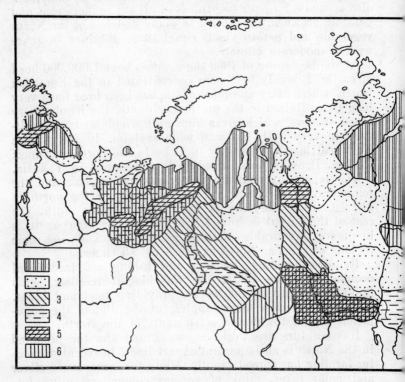

1—reindeer-breeding, hunting and fishing; 2—hunting and fishing; reindeer breeding, hunting and fishing; 5—suburban (dairy farming, vegetabl

reaches of the Kolyma and Indigirka were developed. On the whole, however, communications are still poorly developed.

The territory of the European North is served by three major North-South railway lines—the Murmansk, Northern (Arkhangelsk) and Pechora railways—linked by a number of lateral lines. The network of permanent motor roads is also extensive. In the Asiatic North until recently there were only two small railways—the Chum-Labytnangi, extending for 250 km and linking the Pechora Railway with the lower reaches of the Ob, and the Norilsk-Dudinka railway, extending for just over 100 km and linking the

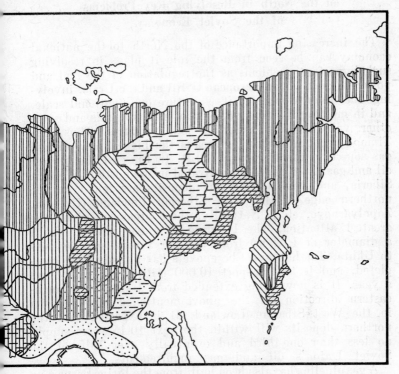

eding; 3—hunting and fishing, stock-breeding, reindeer-breeding; 4—stock-
wing, poultry-breeding); 6—stock-breeding, crop-farming

big industrial centre of Norilsk with Dudinka, the sea
and river port in the lower reaches of the Yenisei. Recently
two new railways were built, the Ivdel-Ob and the Tyumen-
Tobolsk railways, which form the first section of a line
to Surgut, the oil centre in the West Siberian Lowland.
As yet there are no other railways in the whole vast territory
of the Asiatic North. There are few permanent roads, their
place being taken by seasonal forms of transport (thus
the rivers serve for water transport in the summer months
and for motor transport when frozen) and air transport.

2. The Role
of the North in Resolving Key Problems
of the Soviet Economy

The increasing importance of the North to the national economy can be seen from the role it plays in resolving such important problems as the regulation of the fuel and power balance of the European USSR and the Urals, involving the improvement of its structure on a national scale, and in meeting the demand for non-ferrous metals and some other valuable raw materials and products. Thus, the Timano-Pechora oil-bearing area is the biggest new oil and gas source in the European USSR. In the east the biggest oil and gas deposits are concentrated in the north of Western Siberia, and vast natural gas deposits are found on the northern edge of the West Siberian Lowland (Urengoi, Zapolyarnoye, etc.). Naturally, these areas are given the greatest attention. The building of a gas pipeline (with a diameter of 1.22 m) from the big Vuktyl gas deposits to Ukhta, Torzhok and Cherepovets has already been completed, and is to transport 10,000 million cu. m. of gas a year. It is now being extended from Ukhta in a north-eastern direction to the above-mentioned gas deposits in the West Siberian Lowland. It is expected that the northern deposits will within the next 10-15 years supply no less than one-third and eventually over half, of the Soviet Union's oil and gas requirements.

A gas pipeline has also been built from the Igrim-Beryozovo deposits to the Urals to Chelyabinsk, where it links up with Gazli (Central Asia)-Urals pipeline, so that in a few years the Urals will be supplied with gas from these huge northern deposits, from which a gas pipeline now under construction will run to Beryozovo.

The extensive utilisation of northern gas in the industrialised regions of the European USSR and in the Urals is extremely economical. Suffice it to say that the gas from the West Siberian Lowland reaching the Urals costs less than half of that coming from Central Asia, and that its supply to the European USSR, replacing the coal from the Donets basin, will cut fuel costs by about 50 per cent. The utilisation of gas will cut the production costs of many enterprises. For example, the use of gas in open-hearth furnaces lowers coke consumption and increases the yield of metal per square metre of the furnace. It will make it possible to considerably increase the production of metal without additional capital investments and to some extent lower its cost.

The amount of natural gas conveyed from the Timano-Pechora area and the north of the West Siberian Lowland to the industrialised regions of the European USSR and the Urals will within the next few years be equivalent to the amount of coal supplied by the Donets coalfields, at present the main fuel base of the European USSR. The supply of a sufficient amount of cheap fuel opens up wide vistas for the further economic development of the European USSR and the Urals, where the majority of the population and industry are concentrated.

The gas from the Ob North will also exert a major influence on the economic development of the West Siberian economic region. Gas from the Central Ob deposits will be supplied to Novosibirsk, Kemerovo and other regions. As technological fuel it will be about 50 per cent cheaper than the coal from the Kuznetsk basin. As a chemical raw material it will be indispensable in the relevant industries, and it will also play a major role as domestic fuel.

The exploitation of the oil deposits in the two above-mentioned northern oil-bearing areas will be no less important economically. In the Ukhta region, oil production will within the next few years increase 2-3-fold, and part of it is to be transported to Leningrad Region. A large deposit of oil has been discovered in the Usa River basin. However, the West Siberian Lowland will supply the bulk. The recently built Shaim-Tyumen and Ust-Balyk-Omsk oil pipelines have already become operative. The Omsk oil refinery, which until recently operated on Bashkirian oil, has now been transferred fully to northern oil. Within the next 2-3 years oil from the West Siberian Lowland will fully cover Siberia's oil requirements. The oil from the Ural-Volga oil-bearing area will thus be fully utilised in the European USSR. Huge quantities of oil from the North will subsequently be supplied to the Western regions; and a large share will be exported. Giant chemical plants, processing northern oil and gas, are to be set up to the south of the Trans-Siberian Railway and in the Angara-Yenisei region, where cheap hydropower is available.

The production of northern gas will make it possible

to divert much of the Central Asian gas to fulfil local requirements in an area where conditions favour the development of the chemical industry and the need for cheap fuel is great, thereby promoting the further industrialisation of the Central Asian republics.

The vast assessed reserves of natural gas (13,000,000 million cu. m.) in the Yakutia oil-bearing area raise the problem of how that gas is to be delivered to the south of the Far East. Estimates show that it would be economical to build a gas pipeline from the deposits in the mouth of the Vilyui River in the southern Far East, where a plant could be built to liquefy it and export it to the countries of the Pacific. The question of building a pipeline to supply that gas to Eastern Siberia is also under discussion.

It is clear from the above that the oil and gas of the North will play a major role in the economy of the whole country.

The North already holds a leading place in the USSR in the production of non-ferrous metals, gold, diamonds and some other valuable mineral raw materials. With the discovery in recent years of new deposits, unique as regards the concentration of the ores and high useful content, its role has further increased. Among these are the polymetallic ore deposits in Norilsk Region, the Gorev lead and zinc ore deposits near the mouth of the Angara River, the Udokan copper deposit in the north of Chita Region, the tin and gold deposits in the North-East, the titanium deposits in the Komi ASSR, the cyanite deposits on the Kola Peninsula, and many others.

The forests of the North are also of enormous importance to the development of the Soviet economy.

We have noted above the historically conditioned lack of correspondence between the territorial distribution of the forest areas and the places where timber is mainly consumed. Thus, about 50 per cent of the Soviet Union's total timber reserves are in the North, while up to 80 per cent of the timber is consumed in the southern areas, where timber is generally at a premium. In the past decades timber production has decreased in Moscow, Ivanovo, Voronezh, Leningrad, Kalinin and other regions in the central and southern parts of the country, where the forests have been seriously depleted. Water-protective forest zones have been established in those regions. At the same time the development of the forest areas in Arkhangelsk, Vologda and Perm regions, the Komi ASSR, Karelia and other densely forested regions of the European North has been intensified. In addition, millions of cubic metres of timber are supplied to the European USSR from Siberia's remote regions.

A long-range programme has been drawn up for the development of the pulp-and-paper, wood-chemistry and timber processing industries, and it is now being implemented in all densely forested parts of the USSR. The building of a number of pulp-and-paper mills is being completed in the European North, and existing ones are being expanded.

At the same time an extensive programme for the industrial development of the forests in Siberia and the Far East is being carried out, especially in the basins of the Angara River and the northern Ob. Big timber processing mills are under construction there, which make a maximum use of the available timber. The geographical centre of the timber industry is gradually moving eastward, notably to the Asiatic North, where the main timber reserves are concentrated. Eventually Siberia will become the country's main timber exporting region.

Such, in brief, are the main problems linked with the utilisation of the natural resources of the Soviet North. The vast resources in that area determine the scale and trend of development there.

CHAPTER THREE
ASPECTS OF DEVELOPMENT

1. The Development of the North and the Rational Distribution of the Productive Forces

The vast natural wealth of the USSR is extremely varied in kind, concentration, accessibility and effectiveness of utilisation. Naturally, the raw materials and power sources that can, at a given time and with given equipment, be used to the best effect, are developed first. This selectivity in the utilisation of natural resources is practised in all the regions of the country, but particularly in the North, where the severe natural conditions, sparse population and poorly developed transport network make their development particularly difficult.

To make sure that the choice is a correct one, there must be a criterion of effectiveness. Under capitalism this criterion is the rate of profit. The higher the rate of profit and the sooner it can be obtained, the more effective (profitable) is the development of the given natural resource. Effectiveness is considered from the viewpoint of the owner of some enterprise—whether a single owner or a group of owners. Their interests, however, frequently fail to coincide with those of other groups of entrepreneurs and, what is most important, with the interests of the national economy as a whole. In that case the profit of the private owner may turn into a loss for the state as a whole.

In the Soviet Union, where the entire economy is managed according to a single state plan, the criterion of economic effectiveness is advantage to the national economy.

Naturally, in choosing the object for development the expected profitability is always taken into account. There

are, however, cases when new enterprises, or a new transport artery, may operate at a loss at first and yet offer
tangible advantages to the national economy as a
whole, and begin to operate profitably at a later
stage.

The opening up of the Northern Sea Route is a case in
point. Big investments had to be made to study the Arctic
seas, to create a fleet of transport vessels and ice-breakers,
to build ports, etc. Freight transport along that route is
much more expensive than transportation in seas that are
ice-free all the year round, if the operation of the ice-breakers
is taken into account. For a long time the Northern Sea
Route was unprofitable as a transport enterprise. However,
it was not unprofitable when considered from the point
of view of the national economy as a whole. As well as
being a matter of general state importance, the passage
through the Arctic seas has helped in the study of the remot-
est northern territories of the USSR, where many valuable
minerals have been discovered and some are being utilised.
Moreover, the organisation of navigation in the Siberian
rivers that flow into the Arctic seas has made it possible
to penetrate the Far North of the continent, thus promoting
its development.

If we were to compute all the advantages obtained by the
Soviet economy from tapping the riches of the North, which
is connected with the exploitation of the Northern passage,
and were to compare them with the expenditure involved,
we should find that it has proved to be a sound economic
proposition. The route itself also became profitable as soon
as technology advanced and the freight turnover increased.
First to become profitable was the route through the Kara
Sea by which millions of tons of cargoes are transported.
The shipping lines operating in the Northern Sea Route
now not only cover costs but also make a handsome
profit.

The development of new territories is essentially a question of distributing the productive forces in the most rational
way. The industrial development of every new raw material
and power source, just as the building of any new enterprise,
affects the distribution of the relevant branch of production
and also of the productive forces in the region in which it is
located, as well as the inter-regional links, since its operation also has an impact on the economy of other regions.

The changes are the greater, the bigger the new project is, and, hence, the greater the influence it exerts on the national economy.

A look at the history of the transformation of the Soviet Union from a backward agrarian country, which tsarist Russia was, into a great industrial power, shows that the process of industrial development was simultaneously a process of constant change and rationalisation in the distribution of the productive forces.

Industrialisation involved not only the development of the old industrial regions in the Centre and South, but also the intensified development of new regions—the South-East of the European USSR, the Urals, Siberia, Central Asia, Kazakhstan, the Far East, and the North. Industry in the new regions was developed on the basis of the known and newly discovered natural resources essential to the country's advancing economy. Thus, the Urals became a major ferrous and non-ferrous metallurgy and engineering centre. Today the Urals account for one-third of the country's iron and steel production. The oil- and gas-bearing area discovered in the Ural-Volga region accounts for a large share of the oil and gas extracted in the Soviet Union. Big engineering centres have been set up in the Volga regions, a new powerful coal and metallurgical base, a chemical industry and engineering centre have mushroomed in Western Siberia, and the newly discovered rich oil and gas deposits in the northern part of Western Siberia are being developed. Heavy industry has been established in Eastern Siberia, and an all-Union base of power-intensive industries of unprecedented capacity is now being formed there. The Far Eastern regions of the USSR are likewise developing apace.

The changes in the distribution of the Soviet Union's productive forces are proceeding in accordance with the economic laws of socialism. The basic economic law of socialism—the law of the continuous growth and improvement of socialist production on the basis of superior techniques for the purpose of satisfying to the fullest the constantly growing material and cultural requirements of the whole of society—determines the need to draw ever new raw material and power resources into economic use. The law of the planned development of the national economy leads to the establishment of correct proportions between the branches of production in the economy as a whole, and also in each economic region. This secures the co-ordinated development of all regions. The law of value exerts its influence on the correct choice of development projects from the viewpoint of their maximum economic effectiveness.

The above general economic laws of the development of socialist society are the governing principles underlying the rational distribution of the productive forces: bringing industry close to the sources of raw materials, bringing fuel to the areas of its consumption, the specialisation and co-ordinated development of economic regions, more uniform distribution of industry throughout the country, the industrialisation and development of all economic branches in national regions, and the strengthening of the country's defence capacity.

The criterion for the rational distribution of the productive forces is the economy of social labour, the growth of its productivity at all stages from the extractive to manufacturing processes and transportation of the finished product to the consumer. In other words, the criterion is the maximum advantage to the entire economy of the country as well as to its separate parts.

Therefore, in determining the site of a new enterprise, i. e., in deciding whether it should be located in close proximity to the raw material source, the fuel source or the region of consumption, preference is given to the solution that secures the greatest economy of social labour, taking into account the total costs, including those of associated branches of production.

Regional specialisation where the output is intended not only for local consumption, but chiefly to supply other regions, involves a region in the inter-regional division of labour. The choice of the industries in which a region is to specialise is determined in every single case by the conditions favouring such specialisation, ensuring higher productivity of social labour in this particular industry than can be achieved in other regions.

To secure co-ordinated development an optimum "set" of ancillary enterprises must be created to supply the specialised industries of the given region and satisfy the requirements of the local population. The proportions of the branches of production are fixed so as to provide the maximum advantage in the given conditions both to the regional and to the national economy.

The rational distribution of industry is of great importance to the country's defence capacity. This was strikingly demonstrated during the Great Patriotic War (1941-1945), when owing to their industrialisation the Urals and Siberia became the arsenal of the Soviet Army and played an enormous role in securing victory. The utilisation of the northern resources has also contributed greatly to the economic development of the Soviet Union and to the strengthening of its defence potential.

In recent years much attention has been given in the Soviet Union and abroad to quantitative comparisons of different models of production distribution with a view to choosing the optimum solution. Economico-mathematical methods and electronic techniques are widely applied.

The indices of cost price and capital outlay per unit of production are widely used in making a comparative economic assessment of different building projects and determining the effectiveness of the capital outlay. However, these indices do not fully reflect the expenditure of social labour and cannot always be regarded as decisive, since they only provide an approximation of the effectiveness.

In deciding the question of what new natural resources should be exploited, the balance of production and consumption for the given product is of great, sometimes even decisive, importance.

In the scientific planning of the socialist economy estimation of the production-consumption balance is important for establishing correct proportions (ratios) between the different kinds of production, both on a national and economic-regional level. A production balance showing a deficit of some product is a danger signal, for the deficit may arrest the development rates in the branches of production depending on that product or cause other losses to the national economy. Where a balance shows a deficit, it is essential to take into account also the negative effect exerted by the shortage of the relevant raw material or product and the effect the development of the project will have, i.e., whether it will help to abolish or decrease the deficit in its production-consumption balance.

Balance considerations do not only determine the utilisation of natural resources in short supply. Thus, for example, the exploitation of the timber resources in the central and southern regions of the country requires a much smaller labour expenditure than is needed in the European, let alone the Asiatic North. Yet, the development of the forest regions of the North is economically effective and necessary to the development of the Soviet economy. In this case effectiveness is determined not only by a direct comparison of the capital expenditure and cost per unit of output, but also, and indeed mainly, by the fact that the timber resources in the central and southern regions of the country have been largely exhausted and excessive felling over a long period of time leads to the silting up of rivers, may have an adverse effect on climate and produce other negative phenomena detrimental to the national economy and the people's living conditions.

When a comparative assessment demonstrates that it is inexpedient to develop some raw material or fuel base in the North, this does not mean that it will never be exploited. It simply means that at the present economic and technological level the problem can be resolved with a smaller outlay of social labour by using other sources of the same raw material or fuel. Thus, it is as yet inexpedient to set up a big iron and steel centre in the Nizhnyaya Tunguska region, where big deposits of high-quality iron ores and coking coals have been found. At present the iron and steel industry is developing in the more southerly areas of Western Siberia. However, as the national economy develops and when, for example, the output of pig iron will have considerably exceeded the figure laid down for the next 15-20 years, the utilisation of the iron ores and coking coals of the Nizhnyaya Tunguska may become economically expedient. Nor is it to be excluded that in the near future iron ores will be exported from the region by sea to countries where such ores are in short supply.

Thus, in every single instance that a comparative economic assessment is made of the rationality of developing certain natural resources, the question must be considered comprehensively and account must be taken of all the positive and negative influences this development will have on the national economy as a whole.

2. Factors Affecting the Development of the North

The distribution of production among the various economic regions or economic zones is influenced by the specific natural and economic conditions of those regions. The natural environment and economico-geographic position of the different areas loom large among the factors promoting or obstructing the industrial development of the North.

The natural environment exerts a continuous influence on the material life of human society. The industrial specialisation of a region and the creation of the appropriate industries depend on the presence there of certain mineral resources, timber, fuel or water resources, favourable soil and climatic conditions. Differences in the natural environment create a natural basis for the social division of labour between countries and different regions within a country. Because of these differences, even if all other conditions were equal (an identical mode of production and technological level, a similar economico-geographic position, an identical population density, etc.), the manufacture of the same product would require a different labour expenditure in different regions. In regions enjoying more favourable natural conditions the labour expenditure per unit of the same product will be smaller than in regions with less favourable natural conditions, that is, the labour productivity will be higher. In a planned economy a maximum increase in the productivity of social labour can be achieved through the specialisation of every economic region in the kind of output for which it has the most favourable conditions.

The Soviet North has a wealth of natural resources. However, the extremely harsh climatic conditions, in conjunction with the almost universal spread of permafrost, greatly hamper the building and operation of industrial enterprises, complicate the operation of transport, and require the construction of dwellings of a special type. The long winter leaves little time for navigation on the rivers and the ice-bound seas, especially in the Arctic seas through which the Northern Sea Route passes, and this inflates the running costs of the river and sea fleet. The harsh climate makes open-cast mining seasonal, hampers the development of agriculture and, especially in high latitudes, involves

The reindeers in the Chukotka tundra consider helicopters part of the scenery

A veterinary surgeon on an inspection tour to a reindeer-breeding team of a Nenets collective farm

The Pashnya oilfield in the Komi ASSR

The gas collecting centre on the Vuktyl. This is where the Siyaniye
Severa gas pipeline starts

The Norilsk nickel plant, one of the main enterprises in the Arctic town of Norilsk

The Siyaniye Severa gas pipeline under construction

Building of the Khantaika hydroelectric power plant, the world's northernmost. View of the main building. The plant was completed a year ahead of schedule and began to generate power in November 1971

A convoy of vessels breaking through the ice in the Kara Sea

Ships wintering in the Arctic port of Tiksi

An EKG-4.6S excavator loading ore onto a 27-ton Belaz 540S dump-truck. These machines are specially adapted for low temperatures and permafrost

Building of the Vilyui hydroelectric power station. The first
power generating units started operating in 1968

Engine room of the Vilyui hydroelectric power station

a much greater expenditure on the reproduction of labour power (a diet with a higher calory content, more warm clothing, etc.), so that higher wages must be paid[1].

The regions of the North are also remote from industrial centres which could serve as a basis for their development and from the regions where the output is consumed. Transport is poorly developed. There are few motor roads functioning all year round and throughout much of the northern territory seasonal water transport, motor transport along ice roads and animal-drawn transport are the principal means used for the mass transfer of goods. Main railway lines are confined to the European North.

However, the economico-geographic conditions can be changed by man. The setting up of a transport network, of big power stations producing relatively cheap electric power, fuel bases, the industrial development of adjacent districts, and, hence, the bringing closer of bases from which the industrial development of the new territory can be carried out, transform the North. Thus, the building of the Pechora Railway radically altered the economico-geographic position of the Pechora coalfield and the Ukhta oil-bearing area; and the natural resources of the north-eastern part of the Komi ASSR have now been made accessible for industrial development. This applies especially to the goldfields in the upper reaches of the Kolyma and Indigirka, where industrial development could begin only after the port in Nagayevo Bay and the Kolyma motor road had been built.

To overcome the negative effects of the natural environment in the northern territories more social labour must be spent on the building and operation of industrial enterprises, transport development and agriculture, than in other, more southerly areas. At the same time there are a number of reasons why it would be illogical to let the vast natural wealth of the Soviet North go untapped.

Firstly, the numerous valuable mineral deposits in the North are much richer than similar deposits in other parts of the country. The North compares favourably with other

---

[1] The fixing of higher wages for industrial and other workers in the Far North and in regions considered on a par with them is also a measure aimed at drawing people from other regions enjoying more favourable climatic conditions to take part in the development of the North.

areas in the exceptionally high useful content of the ores and placer deposits, the volume of oil and gas deposits, and the bedding of the minerals. Notably, at the Talnakh copper-nickel deposit near Norilsk the useful content is much higher than in the South Urals deposits, and the gold content in the deposits of the northern Chukotka goldfields is several times higher than in many deposits in other parts of the country. As a result the volume of work per unit of output is much lower.

Secondly, many kinds of valuable natural resources, some of them in short supply, are concentrated predominantly in the North.

Thirdly, seemingly negative factors such as low winter temperatures and permafrost, help in some cases to lower the social labour expenditure. Thus, in many places the rivers become improvised motor roads in winter. Permafrost facilitates mining in that there is less ground water, and less propping-up is needed in drifts. The construction of buildings on piles driven to a considerable depth into the permafrost was first tried in Norilsk. Such foundations turned out to be very reliable and reduced the cost of laying foundations in the North to the same level as in the country's central regions.

Many similar examples could be given. They show that modern science and technology make it possible to reduce the effects of the unfavourable aspects of the natural conditions in the North, and make use of favourable aspects.

3. Special Features
of Development of the North

A) *"Nuclear"* or *"Oasis"* *Development of the Natural Resources.* For the development of the natural resources of the North to be economically expedient the positive factors must outweigh the negative factors. The latter are expressed in the cost-raising factor, which is a coefficient determining the increase in the cost of all work carried out in the North. This makes it necessary to give priority to the development of natural resources possessing qualities that decrease the volume of work per unit of output and thus lower the cost of production and the capital outlay. On the whole, it may be said that the development of the natural wealth in the northern regions is economically expedient in the following cases:

1) when, despite the cost-raising factors applying in the North, the valuable properties of the given kind of natural wealth (higher metal content in the ores and placers, higher yields of oil and gas wells, superior bedding, etc.) make the productivity of social labour equal (or higher) to that in the regions of traditional settlement;

2) when this development is dictated by the need of the country's economy for certain raw materials that are unavailable (or lacking) in other parts of the country. In other words, when the losses linked with the short supply of a raw material are higher than the additional expenditure incurred in obtaining it in the North.

The choice of the region that is to be given development priority is not confined to a comparison between North and South. A comparative economic assessment is also made of different regions of the North, which differ as regards natural conditions and geographic location. Obviously, where these regions have identical kinds of natural wealth, preference is given to the one in which an identical effect can be gained with the least social labour expenditure.

Typical of economic development in the North is the prior development of the extractive industries, and the subsequent gradual establishment of processing industries. This is explained by the low population and high costs of development projects. While the share of the North in overall Soviet industrial output is about 3 per cent, in the case of the extractive industry it is over 10 per cent, and for certain products between 30 and 70 per cent. The great distances between raw material deposits and the places where they can be processed make it necessary to set up dressing plants and refineries near the deposits. The concentrates are then transported for further processing to the economically developed regions, sometimes over great distances. Only in exceptional cases are the raw materials fully processed on the spot. As a rule, the processing industry emerges only when a region has reached a higher stage of development, although in certain cases it is economically expedient to create a single complex combining extractive and processing industries. It has been estimated that it is far more economical to process timber fully on the spot, in the direct vicinity of the raw material source, than it is to transport it elsewhere, especially where great distances are involved. In this connection a programme has now been launched for the building of pulp-and-paper mills and wood-chemical plants in forest areas.

In Murmansk Region, where cheap hydroelectric power is available, it is also expedient to process the copper-nickel ore on the spot.

Conditions are far more complicated in Norilsk. The power-intensive complete cycle of nickel and copper production relies on expensive local coal. Conditions are being created for radically reducing the cost of fuel and electric power: a gas pipeline from the Messoyakha is already delivering gas to Norilsk, on the left bank of the Yenisei the first units of the Khantaika hydroelectric power station have been commissioned.

On the whole, at the present level of scientific and technological progress there are no economic prerequisites for the development in the North of a processing industry operating on raw materials brought in from other parts of the country. For example, it would be uneconomical to develop engineering with a view to delivering products to other parts of the country. Only in the European North, which is relatively well-developed economically, do conditions favour ship-building (to supply vessels for the Arctic seas) and engineering (to provide timber felling and processing equipment). In the Asiatic North an exception is represented by Magadan Region, where gold-washing machinery is produced. In all other regions of the North it is only economically expedient to create enterprises for the repair of various kinds of machinery and equipment manufactured in other regions. But here too it should be limited mainly to current repairs, notably the replacement of separate units with similar parts manufactured elsewhere.

The same applies to many branches of the light, food and other processing industries.

Because of the above limitations there are few industries in which the northern regions can specialise. The range of resources being developed is the narrower, the remoter a region and the less accessible as regards transport facilities. This is because their utilisation involves a greater expenditure of social labour and takes longer to recoup. Conversely, the improvement of communications between a particular northern region and other regions of the country, especially the development of railways, extends the range of the raw materials being developed there. Thus, the regions of the North situated comparatively close to major industrial centres or linked to them by good communications (for example, the territories in the European North with a satisfactory transport system) supply a comparatively wide range of raw materials, including timber, coal, oil, iron ore, ferrous and rare metals, apatites, fish, etc. The remoter regions of the Asiatic North, however, supply only a narrow range of easily transportable, valuable metals and minerals—gold, tin, nickel, diamonds, etc.

Since the above specific features favour the priority development only of few valuable mineral deposits or groups of such deposits, and only of the most conveniently located and valuable stands of timber, the building of industrial centres (forming as it were "nuclei" or "oases" in the unpopulated or sparsely populated and practically undeveloped wastes) has become the typical method of development in the northern territories.

These industrial nuclei are many hundreds of kilometres apart, and generally have no economic links with one another, especially in the initial stages of their development. Vorkuta, Norilsk and many other industrial centres are such nuclei. Various industries catering for the needs of the main branches of industry and also for the material and cultural needs of the population gradually form around these nuclei.

Some industrial nuclei gradually become localised industrial districts, large territories being drawn into intensive industrial development of the natural resources. One of these is the Aldan mining area, where many mining enterprises have been set up in the zone orientated towards the Amur-Yakutia motor road, and the Upper Kolyma goldfield, orientated towards the Kolyma motor road.

This "oasis" method of tapping the natural resources lends special features to the structure of the transport network in the northern regions and of the productive forces in general.

B) *Co-ordinated Development*. The economic structure of any region always includes two groups of industries. The first comprises the industries in which the region specialises and which determine its place in the inter-regional division of labour, while the second includes auxiliary and servicing enterprises, whose task is to secure the continuous operation of the specialised branches and to cater for the requirements of the population.

A region's balanced development depends on a correct combination of these two groups of industries, and on rational links and optimal proportions between them. A wrong, economically unjustified selection of branches of the first and the second groups, i.e., a wrong combination of industries in the region, upsets the balance and is harmful to the national economy.

Naturally, economic structures differ from place to place and at different stages of the development of the productive forces in the same region, territory or republic. The range of industries and the extent to which those of the second group are developed depends on numerous factors, notably the requirements of the first group of industries and of the population, resources, raw materials and power sources available locally, communications and the region's level of economic development.

We have frequently had occasion to note that a narrow range of industries is typical of the North, especially of the Asiatic part. We have also examined the reasons for this. The economic expediency of developing the industries of the second group is determined, as in the case of the specialised branches, on the basis of a comparison of the technological and economic indices of factories producing identical output in other parts of the country. The estimates take into account all production costs as well as the cost of delivery to the place of consumption. Such estimates establish whether it is a better economic proposition to produce a certain item on the spot or to bring it from other regions.

It should be pointed out that when a comparative assessment is made of the auxiliary branches of production in northern regions (especially in the Asiatic North), it is generally found that objective conditions make it more expensive to produce the necessary articles on the spot. In addition to such factors as we have already mentioned— severe climate, remoteness from economically developed regions, etc.—there are three factors responsible for the higher cost of production in the second group of industrial enterprises in the North.

70

1. *The small size of enterprises.* Since the population in the North is small and scattered over a vast area, the demand for the output of the servicing and auxiliary branches is relatively small. As a result, it is rarely possible to set up big well-equipped enterprises, even though they generally operate more economically. It is only when a higher stage of development has been reached and there is a big demand for the output of the servicing branches that large enterprises producing only a very limited range of articles can be established. Examples of the latter are the ship-repair yards in Murmansk Region, the repair yards in Magadan and Kamchatka regions, and enterprises catering to the needs of the population of such towns as Murmansk. However, small repair workshops, small enterprises for the production of consumer goods, building materials, etc., will remain typical of the vast and sparsely populated territories of the Far North for a long time to come.

2. *Lack of Local Raw Materials for Certain Consumer Industries.* In most northern regions the very limited produce from animal farming, fishing and hunting are the only raw materials that can be processed locally. Most light industries therefore have to rely on raw materials brought from far away.

3. *Labour-Intensiveness and High Production Costs.* The fact that factories of the auxiliary branches in the North are small and inadequately equipped makes their output very labour-intensive; this, together with higher wages, makes for high production costs.

However, the above limiting factors are not immutable. Thus, for example, at small enterprises, too, a high level of mechanisation and automation can be attained. Moreover, a number of small enterprises can be merged, which, in conjunction with the mechanisation of arduous production processes, greatly raises labour productivity and lowers production costs.

Yet, it would be uneconomical to produce the bulk of the light and food industry products in the North, and it is much more advantageous to ship them from other regions. The range of auxiliary branches it is economically expedient to develop in the sparsely populated northern regions is gradually shrinking as the transport network expands and freight is becoming cheaper.

At the same time it is impossible to close down all the auxiliary enterprises. Some of them have to be run on the spot whatever the economic indices, as being essential to the main specialised industries of the region and its inhabitants. To this category belong the extraction of local fuel (coal, peat), which is needed when it is difficult to supply cheaper fuel (fuel oil, gas) from other regions, the production of electric power, various repair services, bread-baking, the production of confectionery and certain other foodstuffs, agriculture (dairy and poultry farming, stock-breeding to some extent, market gardening, etc.). The additional outlay incurred in the development of these industries in northern conditions is borne by the leading specialised branches and raises their production costs.

Agriculture and local industries occupy a rather special place. Unfavourable soil and climatic conditions make crop farming on a commercial scale impossible, and in many regions this applies also to stock-breeding. The growing of grain and other crops is many times more expensive here than it is in the zones lying further to the south. It is there-fore economically expedient to bring in transportable kinds of agricultural produce from other parts of the country. Only in a few areas—the south of the European North and Central Yakutia—are there "oases", where some grain is grown. The grain provides fodder for dairy cattle, but satisfies the grain requirements of the population only to a very small degree. At the same time the lack of trans-port makes it necessary to organise the production on the spot of highly perishable agricultural products—fresh meat and milk, eggs, vegetables, and in many places pota-toes, too. The experience of some farms and hot-houses shows that such production can be profitable.

Among the traditional occupations of the native popula-tion are reindeer-breeding, hunting and fishing, and in the coastal regions also sealery. The fur industry is one of the economic activities in which the northern regions special-ise. The fur goes to other parts of the country and also for export. Reindeer-breeding supplies the local population and the northern towns with meat (reindeer meat is obtained at less than half the cost of beef). Fishing, except in the Ob basin, is mainly of local importance.

The northern nationalities are scattered over a vast ter-ritory, and even though their numbers are small, they play an important role in tapping the local resources. They are excellent hunters and reindeer-breeders, and in addition to their basic, traditional occupations, participate in geological expeditions, work as guides in inaccessible areas, carry freight on reindeer-drawn sledges, etc. Many young people are employed in industry and transport.

C) *Management.* The "nuclear" development of the northern regions has given rise to special methods of control and forms of economic management. In the developed regions of the country economic management is based on the branch principle, while in remote northern regions, the leading branches of the economy are managed according to the territorial principle. Let us take the example of the Norilsk Copper-Nickel Combine. The combine is in charge of all production and of all the services rendered to the population in the Norilsk industrial centre. It is in charge of a large area which takes in the copper and nickel ore deposits and coalfields and the railway linking Norilsk with the sea and river port of Dudinka on the Yenisei. The plant itself includes a large set of enterprises necessary to ensure the uninterrupted operation of the copper-nickel industry, takes charge of the economic management of the town of Norilsk and the settlements in the surrounding area.

The Vorkuta Ugol (Vorkuta Coal) Combine has an identical structure. It is in charge of many industrial enterprises scattered over an extensive territory, the town of Vorkuta and the settlements near the coal mines. As distinct from Norilsk, which is linked with the outer world only by seasonal transport (by river transport along the Yenisei and by sea transport through the Kara Sea), the Vorkuta Ugol Combine is connected by railway with other parts of the country all the year round.

The structure of the North-Eastern and Yakutia gold combines is slightly different. The former includes all enterprises of the gold, tin and other branches of the nonferrous metal industry in Magadan Region, together with a large number of auxiliary enterprises, and the latter includes all enterprises of the gold, diamond, mica and other mining branches in the Yakut ASSR.

This integrated form of management is necessary because in the remote regions, which are difficult of access for transport, the subordination of every branch of the economy to a different ministry would make it difficult to establish links between them, and would thus interfere with balanced economic development.

Integrated management was introduced in the early stages of the development of the North, when territorial transport-industrial and industrial-transport groups were set up. These included the Transport-Industrial and Settlement Group of the Murmansk Railway (1923-1927), the Komsevmorput Joint-Stock Company under the People's Commissariat for Foreign Trade (1928-1932), the Kamchatka Joint-Stock Company and the Principal Directorate of the Northern Sea Route.

The structure of the groups changed in keeping with the tasks they were called upon to resolve at a given time, local conditions, and the level of economic development. However, they all had definite specific features in common: 1) their activity embraced a strictly defined territory, where all the economic branches and service sectors necessary to resolve the tasks of the group were developed, and 2) the management of all departments of the group was strictly centralised.

In view of the fact that the development in the Far North was restricted to certain areas this form of management made it possible to achieve close co-ordination between the various economic branches there.

D) *Communications.* Transport holds a special place in the development of the productive forces of society. According to Marx's definition it is "a continuation of the production process within the *limits* of the circulation process and *for* the circulation process"; it has an all-embracing character. It helps to carry on the exchange between different branches of production, making them more or less interdependent. The development of the productive forces therefore depends greatly on the development of the transport network.

In the planned economy of the USSR transport not only ensures the conveyance of a steadily increasing volume of freight, but greatly affects the distribution of the country's productive forces. This is particularly evident in newly developed regions, where transport systems are first established and where they make the natural wealth accessible for industrial exploitation. This pioneer role of transport is strikingly manifested in the northern regions, where there are great difficulties involved in drawing them into the country's economic life.

The short summer and long, cold winter, permafrost on a large part of the territory, broken country, the frequent incidence of swamplands, and also the sparse population hamper the building and operation of trunk roads there. Typical of the northern territories is that the freight flows mainly in one direction. Thus, millions of tons are conveyed from the Pechora coal basin and the forest regions of the European North to the south, while the volume of freight from south to north is relatively small. In the Asiatic North the reverse situation obtains. The valuable minerals such as gold, tin and diamonds that are mined there do not weigh much so that the freight (in terms of weight) flows predominantly from south to north.

As we noted above the water transport system of the North is characterised by a very short navigational season. Moreover, the mouths of most northern rivers contain shallow bars, which makes it necessary to carry out loading and unloading operations on the roadstead. The mouth of the Yenisei, where ships with a big displacement are able to sail for a long distance up-river, forms the exception.

For the above reasons the fleet has to lie idle during the long winter and cargoes have to be transferred from sea-going vessels to river vessels and vice versa, entailing considerable additional expense. As a result, the transportation of cargoes by river costs several times more in the northern regions than on rivers in the more southerly areas.

The Northern Sea Route passes through the Kara Sea, the Laptev Sea, the East Siberian and Chukotsk seas, which are situated within the limits of the broad Eurasian continental shelf. The main feature of this sea route is that heavy ice often impedes navigation even during the summer, which only lasts 90-100 days. Because of the small number of deep bays, ships are generally loaded and unloaded on roadsteads. The deep water ports of Dikson and Pevek are the exceptions.

The shortness of the navigation season and the frequent changes in the ice situation make necessary the timely and efficient co-ordinated operation of all units, including the ice service, which forecasts the ice conditions on a route being followed by a vessel. The ports of origin and the Arctic ports, and the entire sea fleet have to work no less efficiently. Powerful technical means have to be used to fight the ice. All this involves a big financial outlay on equipment, on ice-breakers, transport vessels specially designed for Arctic voyages, aviation for ice patrols, meteorological services, etc. The exploitation of the route also incurs additional overheads connected with the maintenance of ice-breakers, the idleness of the Arctic ports during the long winter, expenditure on air patrols and the organisation of pilot services. As a result, freight transport costs on the Northern Sea Route are from 100 to 150 per cent higher than they are on non-freezing seas.

The frosts in winter, snowdrifts and snowstorms obstruct the operation of motor transport. Lorries and spare parts must be of an extra-strong "Arctic design". The operation of vehicles involves a high expenditure of fuel and lubricants, and tyres wear quickly. Since the northern regions are thinly populated, it is extremely difficult to put up snow barriers and to clear the roads of snow. When roads are built in the permafrost zone additional expenditure is incurred by the need to put down a special insulating layer of earth. The building of railways involves similar difficulties. A kilometre of rail or motor road costs from a 100 to 200 per cent more than it does in the central regions of the country. The exploitation of the big motor roads of the North (Kolyma, Amur-Yakutia) shows that even when the freight traffic is well organised and relatively heavy, the cost of freight transfers exceeds the average in the country by no less than 100 per cent.

At the same time the climatic conditions of the North favour the building of temporary winter roads, at only a fraction of the cost of permanent motor roads. In view of the long winter these roads can be used 6 to 7 months a year.

Owing to the enormous distances, especially in the Asiatic North, where there are practically no railways and few motor roads, goods carried by water transport often fail to reach their destination in a single navigational season and remain lying at intermediate warehouses until the next season. It thus takes one and a half to two years for cargoes to reach many of the regions in the North East. This means that stocks have to be put in for a year or more which slows down the commodity turnover.

Air transport depends far less on geographic conditions. That is because all planes flying at high altitudes are designed for low temperatures, and their high speed precludes the delay of cargoes en route, even if vast distances have to be covered. However, mass freight transfers are not yet being handled by air, even though in many cases this would be economical.

Huge territories in the North have no regular communications at all, and special vehicles able to travel over snow and swamps are practically the only transport. The native population and geological expeditions often use reindeer and dog sleighs, which, being light, can follow any trail in the tundra and forest-tundra, and even advance across country having no roads at all. However, such sleighs naturally have a very small freight carrying capacity.

In the European North mass freight transfers are handled by railways, one of the major functions of which is providing inter-regional communications. Railways are built where bulk goods (coal, timber, iron ore, etc.), weighing millions of tons, have to be transported. In several regions of the Asiatic North, the tonnage of the outflow of freight is not big (gold, tin, mica, etc.) and the inflow of goods for production and consumption is much greater (in terms of weight), large shipments, running into the hundreds or even thousands of tons being the rule. This makes it expedient to transport goods by water and roads (including winter roads). Thus, the economic structure in the different regions of the North has a decisive influence on the character of transport.

Each transport system, corresponding to a definite stage of industrial development, is characterised by a certain combination of different forms of transport.

In the economically developed, populated regions of the USSR, which have an extensive, up-to-date transport network, goods are generally moved to or from a particular place along several routes, often parallel, and by several means of transport (railway, road or water), and may be transferred from one to another for parts of the journey. A correct combination of the different kinds of transportation secures a minimum expenditure of social labour on freight transfers.

Things are different in the northern regions, especially in the Asiatic North. Here goods traffic can generally proceed by only one, or at best, two or three routes, which do not run parallel to each other, and which coincide only on some sections. Every route forms a single transport chain, each link being made up of a different means of transport, to which there is no alternative. Thus, for example, freight is delivered to the industrial centre of Deputatsky, between the Yana and the Indigirka, by two main routes: 1) the railways of European USSR to Arkhangelsk or Murmansk, thence by the Northern Sea Route to the mouth of the Yana River, up the Yana to Kuiga and, finally, by the more than 200-km-long winter road to Deputatsky, and 2) by the Siberian railway to Osetrovo (a river port on the Lena River), down the Lena to the port of Tiksi on the coast of the Laptev Sea, by sea to the mouth of the Yana River, and then by the final links of the first route to Kuiga and Deputatsky. Neither of the two routes guarantees the delivery of goods to Deputatsky in a single navigational season. Most cargoes are stored in the warehouses at the mouth of the Yana till the beginning of the next navigation season.

In these conditions the various forms of transport will function smoothly only if the timetables and traffic capacity of all the individual links of the transport chain are properly co-ordinated.

Thus, the timetable of the vessels bringing cargoes to the mouth of the northern rivers by the Northern Sea Route must be strictly co-ordinated with the timetable of the river vessels, whose timetable must in turn be co-ordinated with that for the reloading of the cargoes to lorries at various reloading points upstream. The traffic capacity of the Arctic ports must be co-ordinated with that of the river fleet, and the latter with the traffic capacity of the relevant roads.

While the co-ordination of timetables and the combination of different kinds of transport is essential everywhere, it is of vital importance in the North. Since freight to and from every industrial centre in the Asiatic North can be transported only along one or two routes, and since the navigational season by the water routes, which form major links of the route, is very short, the absence of a co-ordinated timetable or the lack of correspondence in traffic capacity between the various links will inevitably result in long delays en route. This, in its turn, tends to raise transportation costs, since it necessitates transfers by air, the utilisation of roundabout routes and the storage of cargoes, and may occasionally even interrupt the production process and the delivery of supplies for the population.

To make the transport chain in the northern regions more efficient, some forms of transportation are being replaced by others on some sections. For example, for a long time the movement of goods in the Lena basin was only by rough minor roads coming down to the navigable part of the Lena. Their capacity was very small and freight transfers were very expensive. The building of the Taishet-Ust-Kut railway replaced the first link of that route by a more effective means of transportation and improved connections with the Lena basin.

Technological progress makes it possible to find more radical technical and economic solutions to the problem of transport in the remote northern regions which are still difficult of access.

Transport is a region-forming factor: in the North and in some other sparsely populated regions, which are difficult of access, it has a particularly pronounced effect on the formation of economic regions and sub-regions.

In the Far North modern transport arteries designed for mass goods traffic are divided from each other by vast areas where there are practically no communications at all. Under these conditions each of them naturally becomes a centre of the economic life in the contiguous region, and plays a major pioneering role.

The absence of links between the industrially developed regions of the North and the concentration of economic life around transport arteries means that economic regions and sub-regions tend to be closely identifiable with such areas of transport gravitation. This is particularly true in the remote regions of the Asiatic North which are still in the first stages of industrial development.

CHAPTER FOUR
THE IMPROVEMENT
OF ECONOMIC EFFICIENCY

In the preceding chapters we have shown why it is difficult to tap the natural resources of the North. Years of experience in the development of the northern territories and recent scientific and technological achievements, however, indicate that it is possible to considerably reduce the effects of the cost-raising factors in the North and improve economic efficiency in the utilisation of its natural wealth. The successful solution of this task is of enormous importance to the national economy.

The economic development of the northern regions can be made more effective and the productive forces increased only if the expenditure of live labour is economised in all branches.

The remuneration of labour is several times higher in the northern territories than in other parts of the country, being highest of all in the Far North. There are a number of reasons for this.

Firstly, Soviet legislation provides for a wage supplement coefficient for the northern regions of the country. For example, in Murmansk Region the coefficient is 1.5, in Yakutia 1.8, and on the coast of the Arctic Ocean 2. These regional ratings are to compensate for the higher cost of living, resulting from the fact that the severe climatic conditions make necessary a diet including more high-calory foods and a substantial outlay on warm clothing and footwear, and also the fact that because of high transportation costs the prices for some of these goods are 10-15 per cent higher in the North. In addition to regional ratings,

Murmansk. The Lenin Avenue at 3 p.m. when the polar night
is at its deepest

The Zhdanov Avenue in Monchegorsk, the centre of the copper
and nickel industry on the Kola Peninsula

Timber procurement in one of the timber procurement establishments in Arkhangelsk Region

Newsprint made in Kondopoga

The Komi ASSR. A depot of the Tishmer timber procurement establishment

The Komi ASSR. Swimming pool at the Young Pioneers' and Schoolchildren's Palace in the town of Vorkuta

special benefits and supplements have been established to attract workers and specialists to the North, their size depending on the length of service in the North, and also on the remoteness of the region and the severity of its climate. As a result, the total earnings of a worker who has spent several years in the North are two to three times higher than those of a worker of an identical category in the other regions of the country.

Secondly, owing to the specific natural conditions in the North (permafrost, swamplands, severe climate, snowstorms, blizzards, etc.) more effort is required to do a job than would be needed in other parts of the country with the same equipment.

Finally, considerable expenditure is incurred by the organised recruitment of workers and specialists for the North, their passage there and, especially, the creation of the services necessary to ensure normal living and working conditions for them.

On the whole the expenditure on the remuneration of labour on a job in the North is from three to five times higher than that for an identical job in regions with a moderate climate.

It follows that a cut in labour expenditure on a given volume of work provides a much greater saving in expenditure in the northern regions than a similar cut would provide in other parts of the country.

The equipment available to labour plays a particularly important role in the economic utilisation of the labour resources. It will be remembered that the utilisation of machinery is economically effective when the sum total expenditure on its production and operation is lower than the labour it replaces. Since the expenditure on the remuneration of labour is several times higher in the North than it is in other regions, the effect from the utilisation of machinery is also several times higher there. This means that even if it is uneconomical to use some machines in the more developed regions of the USSR, their utilisation may be effective in the North. The fact, that the machinery for the North is manufactured at large-scale modern factories in the economically developed central or southern regions, where there is no additional outlay on labour remuneration, makes it even more important to use highly productive machinery in all the economic branches in the North. For the above reasons, machinery is relatively cheap as compared with human labour, despite the high delivery costs.

High technical equipment presupposes an efficient organisation of labour, and the utilisation of technological schemes in production and construction that afford a maximum economy of labour expenditure. The more severe the natural conditions and the more remote and sparsely populated the developing region, the greater are the effects from the utilisation of highly productive equipment, the mechanisation and automation of production, and the scientific organisation of labour.

At the same time it must be remembered that the utilisation of equipment that is not suited to the special conditions of the North may result in big losses. Mining, building, transport, agricultural and other machinery of standard design wears out two to three times more quickly in the North than it does in the central parts of the country. Ordinary steel and some non-ferrous metals become brittle at temperatures of minus 20°C, and especially below 35°C. The parts and assemblies of machinery working under stress wear out particularly quickly—the handle and bottom of an excavator's scoop, the platforms of big lorries, etc.

Low temperatures decrease the productivity of lorries, tractors, and other equipment not supplied with starter heaters, while, to ensure normal working conditions, the driver's cabin must be hermetically sealed and heated.

In calculating the advantage derived from the utilisation of equipment suitable for Arctic conditions one must consider not only the direct saving (decrease in downtime, volume of repair work, etc.), but also those obtained from reduction of manpower.

Much has been done in recent years in the USSR to create equipment suitable for operation at low temperatures, on frozen soils and in swamplands. Dozens of research institutes and design offices are working to produce various kinds of equipment of special Arctic design. Dozens of different models have been produced and tested, including the highly successful EKG 4.6C excavator, the D572C bulldozer and the D515C ripper. The extra cost involved in their production is recouped in two to six months. The number of people required for their operation is much fewer. A number of machines have gone into mass production and production is underway of frost-resisting steel, lubricating and rubber materials, etc. The output of spare parts has been increased in order to confine repairs to the replacement of quickly-wearing parts and units.

Between November 1968 and March 1969 the All-Union Exhibition of Economic Achievement in Moscow organised the first display of models of Arctic equipment ever to be held in the USSR. The exhibition showed the considerable achievements made in that field. The lorries, excavators, building and road-building machinery, etc., displayed there were of the frost-resistant and sturdy type. In addition to the Arctic modifications of standard machinery, machines specially designed for northern conditions were displayed. It is planned to set up special factories, as well as work-shops and production lines at existing factories, for the mass production of such machinery. Research institutes and design offices are working to create sets of Arctic machines for various purposes: sets of mining equipment, extra-sturdy lorries, road-building machines, etc. The 23rd and the 24th Congresses of the CPSU declared that the creation of machines suitable for work in the natural conditions of the North for all branches of production was an important national-economic task, and that the northern regions would be supplied with such machinery within the next few years.

It should be noted that it is not only a question of equip-ping all the economic branches in the North with various kinds of machinery suited to the climatic conditions there. The high concentration of natural resources also requires that these machines should be extremely powerful. Sturdy and reliable machines require less maintenance and fewer people to service them and are therefore instrumental in lowering the cost of work done, and, what is particularly important, help to accelerate development.

It is generally recognised that the enterprises in the northern regions, where labour is expensive, must be given high priority in the supply of advanced machines, and that the production processes must be highly mechanised and automated. Naturally, the economic branches of the North cannot all be re-equipped at once. New enterprises receive new machinery first. However, the complete re-equipment of the northern economy is to be carried out gradually over the next few years.

At present large funds are still being spent on equipment repairs in the North. Measures are now being taken to organise the production of more spare parts and units in the economically developed regions in order to reduce on-the-spot repairs to the simple replacement of worn-out parts. As regards general and major overhauls, they must be carried out at specially organised "supply bases", which we shall be discussing further on.

Due to the higher labour remuneration, the high cost of the transportation of building materials and a number of other negative factors, the cost of construction work in the northern regions is from one and a half to two times what it is in other parts of the country in the case of large-scale development and from three to five times as much in the case of separate or isolated enterprises, dwellings, etc. This means that the volume of building and assembly work costing say a million rubles in the central regions, will cost between 2 million and 5 million rubles in the North. Since the amount of capital investments for an identical volume of construction work is so much higher in the North, the cost of the fixed assets of enterprises is also much higher. This, in addition to the fact that the service life of buildings in the North is shorter than in other regions, makes for extremely high depreciation deductions and a corresponding increase in the cost of the output.

Construction in conditions where low temperatures, permafrost and swamplands prevail requires special methods corresponding to the different nature of the task. The Soviet Union leads the world in developing methods for construction in permafrost conditions. The building of such towns as Norilsk and Vorkuta is an example of the application of industrial building methods in the most severe natural conditions. Thus, for example, the method of building pile foundations was first employed in Norilsk. Reinforced concrete piles are driven deeply into the permafrost and frozen in. Such foundations are no less durable than rock foundations. The industrialisation of all work has lowered the cost of foundations to such an extent that it does not exceed that of ordinary foundations in central areas of the country.

Industrial methods are used chiefly in areas of concentrated construction and are rarely employed for the building of isolated dwelling houses, public and production buildings.

Such building work is carried on in numerous villages, at mines and goldfields and other enterprises, is practically unmechanised and therefore extremely expensive.

The fact that the transportation of building elements is extremely complicated and expensive makes it economical to reduce the weight of buildings and structures to a minimum by using such materials as plywood, chipboard, polymers and aluminium. Thus, thermo-insulated aluminium panels, brought by air from Irkutsk, were used in the building of the 15-storey ore-dressing factory at Mirny, considerably speeding up construction. The use of foam plastics of polystyrene PS-b greatly reduces the cost of walls.

The setting-up of supply centres for the building industry in the northern regions is generally expedient only in areas of construction where local building materials are available. For small-scale construction, and also for large-scale developments in the remote and sparsely populated regions, it is more rational to have light-weight large-sized blocks and prefabricated building elements sent from industrial centres situated to the south and assembled on the site.

In the north-eastern regions, where many of the placer deposits of gold and tin are exhausted in 5-15 years (depending on the productivity and equipment employed), it is rational to build sectional prefabricated dwelling houses and production buildings, which are easily dismantled when no longer needed. The repeated utilisation of prefabricated structures cuts building costs, while prefabricated-unit technique accelerates construction and improves quality.

An important way of cutting costs and improving construction and repair work in the North is setting up special supply bases, each serving a large area. Technical and economic calculations are made to determine the optimum site for these bases. Enterprises producing building units and elements for sectional construction by industrial methods are being set up there. It is most rational economically to produce reinforced-concrete structures for the regions served by railways or a smoothly functioning water transport system, and structures in light-weight materials (aluminium, thermo-insulated plywood, etc.) where air transport predominates. The prefabricated structures are assembled on the spot, a method which makes a great saving in time and manpower. It is far more profitable to set up such construction bases than to have bases utilising local materials found in the area being developed.

The high efficiency of sectional construction has been proved by extensive pipeline building. This, in particular, explains why the laying of pipelines in the Soviet North is being carried out in record time. Thus, the 1,000-km. Ust-Balyk-Omsk gas pipeline was completed in one year, and the 1,200-km. Vuktyl-Torzhok gas pipeline in a little over a year.

The establishment of construction supply bases where many different auxiliary enterprises are concentrated, helps to rationalise the economic structure of the northern industrial centres.

Large industrial construction bases have recently been set up in Murmansk Region, Karelia and the Komi ASSR, and in the towns of Surgut, Norilsk, Magadan and others. Construction bases are also springing up in regions contiguous with the northern zone, supplying the latter with industrially produced building elements. Such, for example, are the bases in Tyumen and Tomsk.

High transport costs jack up the cost of all jobs carried on in the northern districts. In the Far North, especially where there are no railways, the cost of transporting goods is dozens of times higher than it is in the economically developed regions which have a modern transport network.

This cost increment is linked, firstly, with the enormous distances involved (in some cases 10,000 to 12,000 km.), and secondly, with the fact that expensive forms of transport have to be used in the regions without railways—seasonal water transport, winter roads, and in a few regions, motor transport. In this connection, the reader is once more reminded that the cost of freight transfers by road and water in the North is more than twice as high (on rivers where the goods traffic is small—8 to 10 times higher) as it is by the same kinds of transport in the economically developed regions.

Transport costs in the North can be reduced by building more direct roads and improving the transport "chains" by which goods are delivered, replacing some links of the chain by more economical ones. As we have already noted, the replacement in 1950 of the Zayarsk-Ust-Kut motor road leading to the navigable part of the Lena by the Taishet-

Ust-Kut railway cut the transport costs on that section of the transport "chain" to a fraction of what they had been.

Air transport plays an important role in the Asiatic North, where ground communications are almost totally lacking. Its higher cost there is due mainly to the additional expenditure on building of airfields and other structures, and fuel deliveries. However, this relatively small increment in costs, as compared with regions with a milder climate, is more than compensated by the speed of deliveries. The construction in recent years of freight planes with a high payload has made the air freight transport much more economical. The plane most frequently used in the Soviet North is the ANT-12, with a payload of up to 20 tons; soon the world-renowned Antei will be brought into service on local routes.

The building of big power stations operating on cheap fuel helps to lower additional outlay in the North more than anywhere else. Such power stations are already operational in areas of greatest industrial concentration (in Murmansk Region, Karelia, Norilsk, etc.). The building of relatively big power stations, which are to replace the smaller ones producing expensive electricity, is assuming a large scale. The Arkagalinsk district power station in the centre of southern Magadan Region supplies a vast area with relatively cheap power. In Bilibino, the new centre of the gold-mining industry near the Chaunskaya Guba in the north of the Chukotka National Area, building is nearing completion of a district atomic power station which will be linked up by an electric transmission line with the thermal power station in the port of Pevek, and will supply the whole of the vast territory of western Chukotka. Big power stations are being built in all the regions of the European North, in the West Siberian Lowland and in central Yakutia, where cheap natural gas is used as fuel. Small atomic power stations are justified for regions with small, scattered consumers, such as northern Chukotka.

The industrial development of new big projects in the North requires extensive research work before construction is begun, as well as the creation of the territory's infrastructure—roads, power stations, housing and other structures—without which the main projects cannot be completed in a short time.

Experience has shown that without thorough preliminary

research, construction proceeds more slowly and additional expense is incurred.

In the North, where manpower is in short supply and extremely expensive, it is highly important to attract skilled specialists and workers and to create a permanent labour force there. It will be remembered that when workers are armed with identical equipment, their labour productivity depends largely on the skill with which they operate the equipment. Reducing the labour turnover, still very high in the northern regions, is thus a matter of considerable importance.

Much has already been done in this respect. The decree of the USSR Supreme Soviet in 1967 provided among other things for an increase in the privileges granted to people working in the North, and also for a higher rate of housing construction than in other regions. The directives of the 24th Congress re-emphasised the importance of these measures.

In view of the harsh natural conditions, the inclement weather in autumn and winter (that is, throughout the greater part of the year), frequent hurricane-force winds, snowstorms and frost, the populated centres need to be specially planned to protect people against the rigours of the northern climate. The principle underlying such planning is that the buildings themselves should afford protection against winds, that is, that they should be arranged so as to make the space between blocks of houses a calm zone with a milder microclimate.

Typical in this respect is the layout of the town of Norilsk. Considering that snow and wind penetrate into yards and blocks of houses through the passages between buildings, the designers have reduced their number to a minimum. The façades of tall houses form a shield against wind and snow. They also provide a shelter for the schools, kindergartens and crèches, various service establishments and children's playgrounds built in the space enclosed by the blocks. Even during fierce blizzards people are able to move about there with relative ease.

The figure on p. 89 shows a Norilsk microdistrict (No. 1) with an area of about 24 hectares. It extends along Lenin Avenue. The sports centre and plazas are located in the centre of the microdistrict.

The layout of a new microdistrict (No. 10) differs

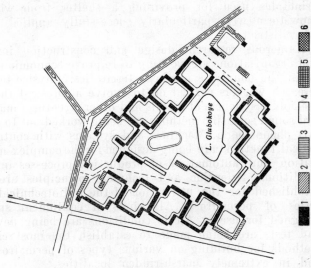

LAY-OUT OF MICRODISTRICT No. 10 IN NORILSK

L. Glubokoye

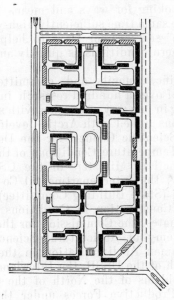

LAY-OUT OF MICRODISTRICT No. 1 IN NORILSK

Typical of Norilsk are yards providing a shelter from blizzards and snowstorms. Schools and kindergartens are built within such enclosures.

1—dwellings; 2—built-in service establishments; 3—recreational establishments; 4—kindergartens, creches; 5—schools; 6—shopping centre from the first in that the designers were not compelled to take into account the previously existing layout. The principles used for providing a shelter from wind and snowstorm were particularly successfully applied in this microdistrict.

Numerous research, design and construction institutes and organisations are working to improve economic efficiency in the country's northern territories. Physico-technical research work is carried on to evolve a physical theory of the cold brittleness of metals and other structural materials, and sound scientific methods are being worked out to combat this phenomenon. Machines and systems with control and logical functions are being designed for the complex mechanisation and automation of production processes in Arctic conditions. Scientific and technical principles are being established for the utilisation of the radiotechnical properties of permafrost. All kinds of equipment specially designed for use in Arctic conditions are being developed and tests are being made to establish the most effective methods for building on various types of permafrost soils and in extremely marsh-ridden localities.

"Arctic biology" is looking for ways and means to grow frost-resistant and at the same time sufficiently high-yielding crops. "Arctic medicine" searches for ways to help people acclimatise to the northern conditions as quickly and painlessly as possible.

A number of scientific councils and committees are co-ordinating the work of over a hundred research institutes and design offices dealing in one way or another with scientific and practical questions linked with Arctic development. Among them is the Scientific Council for the Designing of Machinery for Low Temperature Conditions of the State Committee of the Council of Ministers of the USSR for Science and Technology, the Interdepartmental Co-ordination Council of Gosstroi (State Building Committee) of the USSR for Problems of Construction in Conditions of Permafrost and Severe Climates, the Commission for the North of the All-Union Academy of Agricultural Sciences, the Commission for the Human Acclimatisation in the North of the Ministry of Health of the USSR, the Interdepartmental Commission for Problems of the North of the Council for the Study of the Productive Forces under the State Planning Committee of the USSR.

These organisations regularly call meetings and symposiums at which they review the results of research and practical work, and outline the trends of future research.

A number of branches of the USSR Academy of Sciences are situated in the northern regions—the Kola branch in the town of Apatity in Murmansk Region, the Karelian branch in Petrozavodsk, the Komi branch in Syktyvkar, capital of the Komi ASSR, the Yakutian branch in the town of Yakutsk. Every branch has a number of research institutes, departments and research stations. For example, the Kola branch has a Geological Institute, an Institute for Chemistry and Mineral Raw Materials, a Mining and Metallurgical Institute, a Department for Economic Research, the Murmansk Marine Biological Institute, the Polar-Alpine Botanic Institute in the village of Kukisvumchorr. The Komi branch includes a Geological Institute, a Biology Institute, a Language, Literature and History Institute, Departments of Economics, Chemistry, the Power Industry and the Water Economy, and a Biological Research Station in the village of Vilgort. There are 17 scientific and design institutes in Magadan.

Many thousands of research workers and engineers of different specialities are engaged in studying various problems of the Soviet North. Their efforts are directed towards the single aim of accelerating the utilisation of the vast natural wealth of the Soviet North.

CHAPTER FIVE
THE EUROPEAN NORTH

The northern part of the European USSR, embracing Murmansk and Arkhangelsk regions, the Karelian ASSR and the Komi ASSR, occupies an area of 1,321,000 sq.km., or over a quarter of the territory of the European USSR, and could comfortably accommodate France, Italy and Spain. Yet it contains only 2.9 per cent of the population of the European USSR.

The area forms part of the North-West Economic Region, together with Leningrad, Novgorod, Pskov and Vologda regions, and accounts for four-fifths of its area, about one-third of the population, a quarter of the gross industrial output and over two-fifths of the fixed industrial productive assets. It contains the region's main raw material deposits and fuel resources (apatite-nepheline, copper-nickel and iron ores, titanium, bauxites, coal, oil and natural gas) and the bulk of the timber and fresh water resources. The area is well developed economically and holds an important place in the industry of the North-West Economic Region. Its vast natural resources, and its favourable economico-geographic position, thanks to its railway connections with Leningrad and the central industrial regions of the country, as well as its convenient sea connections, create favourable conditions for its further economic development.

The natural conditions, including the soil and climatic conditions, are less favourable than in the contiguous areas to the south. Agriculture is carried on only in the southern parts of Arkhangelsk Region and the Karelian ASSR and Komi ASSR, and arable lands form oases in an otherwise barren territory. In Murmansk Region, in the northern part of Arkhangelsk Region and the Komi ASSR, reindeer-breeding is carried on on a small scale, but hunting and fishing are developed in all parts of the area.

The economic specialisations are timber and wood-processing (accounting for about one-third of the gross output), non-ferrous metallurgy (nickel), engineering (ship-building and machinery for the timber and wood-processing industry), fuel (coal, oil and natural gas), mining-chemical industry (production of apatite concentrates) and fishing. Over 80 per cent of the industrial workers are employed in these branches, which account for three quarters of the gross industrial output and the productive assets of industry.

Economic links are weak between the autonomous republics and regions that comprise the area but strong with the areas to the south. This is a historically conditioned state of affairs, since the old industrial areas of the Centre, and especially Leningrad Region, formed the base for the industrial development of the natural resources of the European North. Practically the whole output of the branches in which the European North specialises is transported to other regions, notably to Leningrad Region and the central parts of the country. The European North is one of the main suppliers of timber for the whole of the European part of the USSR. Apatite concentrates from Murmansk Region are sent to all parts of the European USSR, especially the Ukraine and Moldavia (over one-third), as well as to the North-West and Centre economic regions; a large share also goes to Central Asia and Kazakhstan. About 50 per cent of the apatite is exported. Iron ore concentrates from Murmansk Region and coking coal from the Pechora coal-fields provide the raw material and fuel for the Cherepovets iron and steel works.

Plant, consumer goods, agricultural produce and oil products and also several million tons of coal are brought in from other parts of the country.

The timber and wood-processing industry is developed in Arkhangelsk Region, the Komi ASSR and Karelian ASSR. Murmansk Region is the centre of mining and chemicals, and the most important base of Soviet fishing industry. Murmansk is the homeport of a vast fleet of traulers which fish in distant Pacific and Atlantic seas. Specialised machine building is concentrated in Arkhangelsk Region and Karelia. The Komi ASSR is famous for its coal, oil and natural gas. As industrial development continues, more and more economic links are being forged between the separate regions which are gradually coming to form a well-knit economic whole. There are three main problems to be solved.

1. The problem of ensuring the rational utilisation of the local raw materials and fuel.

2. The problem of the effects of the discrepancy in the geographic distribution of raw materials and power resources.

3. The problem of making the whole area a single economic unit with a rational structure, and achieving the right combination of the branches of production in which it specialises and various auxiliary branches.

For convenience, the area has been divided into two parts, North-West and North-East.

1. The North-West

General

This area comprises the Karelian ASSR and Murmansk Region. It is linked with the other regions of the country by the Murmansk Railway, the White Sea-Baltic Canal and the sea routes passing through the White and Barents seas.

The Karelian ASSR consists mainly of lowlands, rising slightly at the watersheds (350-400 m.), and is characterised by extensive swamplands and numerous lakes. Murmansk Region occupies the Kola Peninsula. It has several hilly districts, the most considerable of which are the Khibiny and Lovozero tundras with a maximum elevation of 1,200 m. The northern shores of the Kola Peninsula are washed by the non-freezing Barents Sea. The mean January temperature on the coasts of the peninsula is minus 6°C to minus 7°C, and minus 13°C in the centre. To the south of the Kola Peninsula, in Karelia, the mitigating influence of the warm, North Cape current decreases, and the minimum temperatures in Petrozavodsk reach minus 40-50°C in February. The mean July temperatures, on the other hand, are higher here (plus 16.6°C). They drop appreciably on the coast (Murmansk, plus 12.8°C). The mean annual precipitation fluctuates in the northwestern territory between 350 and 650 mm. The snow lies for about seven months. Strong winds combined with frosts and considerable humidity make the climate extremely severe.

On the whole, natural conditions do not favour the development of agriculture, except in the southern part of Karelia, where agriculture has been carried on since early times. Only a few vegetables and potatoes ripen in Northern Karelia and in the Kola Peninsula. There is some dairy farming scattered throughout the area, but not enough to meet local requirements for fresh products.

There are substantial differences between the production specialisation of the Karelian ASSR and Murmansk Region. Karelia is known primarily for its timber and wood-processing industry, which is highly developed there, especially pulp-and-paper (10 per cent of the USSR total). The Karelian Segezha and Kondopoga pulp-and-paper mills are among the biggest in the country. The pulp-and-paper industry uses local hydroelectric power. There is also a developed engineering industry geared to the production of equipment for forestry and wood processing. Heavy lumber tractors for the entire European North are produced in Petrozavodsk, and the first section of a large factory for paper-making machines has been completed there. The fishing industry is important on the shores of the White Sea. The republic is also rich in building materials.

Murmansk Region has extremely valuable mineral deposits, and mining is important, especially for apatite-nepheline and copper-nickel, and iron ore. A large non-ferrous metal and chemical industry has been built up to process these ores. The region is also famed for its fishing industry.

The North-West of the European North is deficient in energy resources. Two small aluminium works are using the water power of the Niva River (Kandalaksha works) and the White Sea-Baltic Canal (Nadvoitsy works). But the water-power resources are limited, although far from being exhausted. A number of hydroelectric power stations are being built in co-operation with Norway and Finland. But the hydroelectric resources of the area, even if used to the full, will not suffice to tap the enormous mineral and other raw material resources of the Kola Peninsula. The small local peat and schungite reserves can only make a negligible contribution to the solution of the fuel problem.

Every year over two million tons of coal have to be brought in, mainly from the Pechora and Donets coalfields and Spitzbergen. The local fuel situation is expected to become more acute as time goes on.

In both Karelia and Murmansk Region, the economically most developed districts gravitate towards the road and railway networks and the White Sea-Baltic Canal. At the same time considerable areas in western Karelia, the eastern part of the Kola Peninsula, and other districts are still weakly developed. However, their natural resources have been well studied and it has been found expedient to exploit them industrially. This applies also to the practically inexhaustible reserves of Keiv cyanites in the eastern part of the Kola Peninsula, the iron ores in western Karelia, etc.

Forestry

Most of the timber reserves are in the Karelian ASSR (1,002.3 million cu.m.). By 1969, 18 million cu.m. a year was being procured, more than ten times the amount in 1913. The timber industry accounts for over 50 per cent of Karelia's total industrial output. As distinct from the other regions of the European North, the Karelian ASSR has not only highly developed saw-milling, but, even more important, a pulp-and-paper industry. Coniferous species account for almost 90 per cent of the total stands. The forests in the south of Karelia are much denser than those in the north, and the timber is of higher quality.

A study of the development prospects of the timber industry in the Karelian ASSR has shown that due to excessive felling in the past, cutting in the southern part should be lowered to about 13-14 million cu.m. a year. At the same time it will be increased substantially in the hitherto little-developed western part of the republic.

Within the next 10 to 15 years the pulp-and-paper and the wood chemical industries will remain the leading branches of the timber-processing industry. The capacity of the mills will be increased and the timber will be put to better use.

The timber resources of Murmansk Region are small, and are mainly concentrated in its south-eastern part. Production runs to about two million cu.m. a year and the timber is processed at local sawmills.

Minerals

Academician A. Y. Fersman's book *Mineral Resources of the Kola Peninsula* reviews the results of geological prospecting carried out over a period of twenty years under his direction, and also the work done by many other scientists. According to Fersman the natural resources of the peninsula can be characterised as follows:

1. A truly gigantic concentration of mineral deposits, lying close to one another.

2. The mineral raw materials have a complex chemical composition, due to the fact that they were formed at exceptionally high temperatures and high pressure.

Fersman names ten powerful geochemical foci of mineral concentration: Notozero, a source for copper, nickel and raw materials for sulphuric acid production; Monchegorsk-Imandra, which is rich in copper and nickel, and iron ore; Knibiny, with its apatite and nepheline; Lovozero, having raw materials for the niobium industry; Yena (Kovdor) with its vast iron ore deposits; Kandalaksha, a source for olivinite, titanium and iron with an admixture of rare metals; Keiv with its vast concentration of cyanites; Tersky, where copper sulphite, mica, tungstenite and other minerals have been discovered; Severny, a source of building and cementing materials, and the upper reaches of the Nota River, where asbestos, talcum, chromites and pegmatites are concentrated. To this list should be added the Pechenga deposits of copper-nickel ores.

Among the numerous minerals found in the Kola Peninsula, Fersman singles out a number of world or all-Union importance as regards the size of the deposits and the quality of the minerals. They include: apatite, the raw material for the production of phosphate fertilisers, and nepheline, the raw material for various branches of the chemical industry and aluminium production, of which there are thousands of millions of tons; cyanites, the raw material for the production of refractory materials and aluminium, of which there are practically inexhaustible reserves; iron ore, of which the assessed reserves in the Yena (Kovdor) deposits alone number thousands of millions of tons; copper and nickel ores, accounting for a sizable part of the total world reserves; rare earths, of which millions of tons are contained in the apatites and loparites; niobium ore; zirconium, olivinites, the raw material for refractory materials, and abrasive garnet of excellent quality.

Fersman notes that 59 chemical elements have been found in the region. A detailed study of the geology of the Kola Peninsula and its minerals has fully confirmed Fersman's conclusions. Many new mineral deposits have been discovered, notably a mica deposit of all-Union significance. As a result of years of research technological plans have been drawn up for the rational co-ordinated utilisation of many different ores. The development of Murmansk Region as an industrial area is favoured by its good rail connection with Leningrad, one of the country's major industrial and cultural centres, proximity to the White Sea-Baltic Canal, the fact that the port of Murmansk is ice-free all the year round and the numerous convenient bays along its shoreline.

For over two decades now the apatite mined at Khibiny in the Kola Peninsula has provided practically four-fifths of the raw material for the production of phosphate fertilisers in the USSR.

The Khibiny apatite ores contain 20-25 per cent of P_2O_5. Their concentrates contain 39.5-40 per cent of P_2O_5. The production cost per ton of P_2O_5 made of Khibiny apatite concentrates is 17.1 rubles, which is 41-61.5 per cent lower than the cost of P_2O_5 made of phosphorite concentrates from the Vyatka-Kama, Yegoryevsk, Kingisepp and Karatau phosphorite deposits. The production of apatite concentrates is increasing apace.

The exploitation of phosphorite deposits in other parts of the country will not lower the share of the Khibiny apatites in the production of superphosphates, or decrease their importance. Their high quality, low production cost and the size of the reserves ensures that their extraction and processing will continue to grow.

All the nepheline and other valuable components contained in apatite-nepheline ores are at present being wasted when apatite concentrates are produced. However, within the next few years nepheline will be widely applied owing to a new technology of extraction and utilisation, which has already been tested on an industrial scale at the Volkhov aluminium mill. The fact that various valuable products—alumina for the production of aluminium, potash, cement, bicarbonates—can be obtained from nepheline, makes it economically expedient to process it.

INDUSTRY IN THE NORTH-WESTERN TERRITORIES OF THE EUROPEAN NORTH

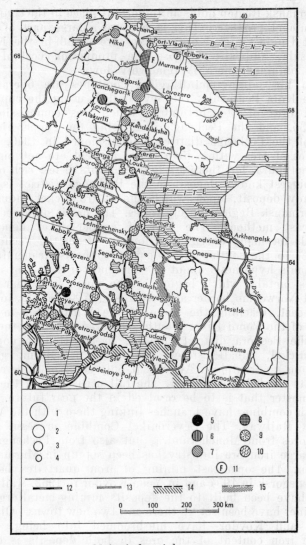

Main industrial centres:
1. very big 2. big 3. medium 4. small
Branches of industry:
5. ferrous metallurgy 6. iron ore extraction 7. non-ferrous metallurgy 8. engineering and metalworking 9. chemical industry 10. timber industry 11. fishing industry 12. Railways 13. Motor roads 14. Southern boundary of the North 15. Boundary of the North-Western Region

Murmansk Region holds an important place in the country as a nickel producer. This is because a large part of the Soviet Union's nickel ore reserves are found in the Kola Peninsula, and also because the production cost of the metal obtained there is relatively low.

Two big mining-metallurgical combines are operating in the Kola Peninsula: the Severonikel, using the copper-nickel ores of Monchetundra, which was commissioned in 1936, and the Pechenganikel, using the copper-nickel ores of the Pechenga district, commissioned in 1946. The reserves of ores with a high metal content are not big in Monchetundra, but there are large deposits of less rich ores. The biggest known deposit in the Pechenga district is the Zhdanov deposit, upon which the entire nickel industry of Murmansk Region largely relies. The ore is obtained by open-cast methods. The belt of copper-nickel deposits extends for many dozens of kilometres from the Pechenga district to the south-east. It partly confirms Academician Fersman's hypothesis about the presence of a belt of non-ferrous metals, which begins in the north-west near the Soviet-Norwegian border and extends for 700-800 km. to the south-east, reaching the shore of the White Sea, to the north of the Ponoi River mouth. The ores of Monchetundra and the Pechora district contain, in addition to copper and nickel, cobalt, silver, platinum, palladium, gold, selenium, and sulphur. At present only some of these components are being extracted. The full utilisation of the ore is a matter that is to be resolved in the near future.

Both combines have branches linking them with the Murmansk Railway. The Severonikel Combine processes not only ores from Monchetundra, but also from Pechenga.

A large iron ore industry has been set up in Murmansk Region. The open-cast mining of iron quartzites began in Olenegorsk in 1954 and in Yena-Kovdor in 1962. Railway lines have been built to the deposits, mining-metallurgical combines have been set up there and two new towns—Olenegorsk and Kovdor—have mushroomed into being.

The iron content of the ores in both deposits is only 30 per cent, but the quartzites contain little sulphur or phosphorus and are therefore easily concentrated. The concentrates contain 60 per cent and more iron and are suitable for smelting. These deposits supply the Cherepovets Iron and Steel Works with raw materials, and some of the concentrates are exported to West European countries. The ores also contain some other valuable components, which are as yet not extracted because the complicated technological processes required for it have not yet been fully elaborated. This is only a matter of time.

The planned increase in the capacity of the Cherepovets Iron and Steel Works has evoked interest in the iron ores of the Kostomuksha deposit in the Karelian ASSR, situated near the recently built West Karelian Railway.

The Kostomuksha deposit, as also the deposits in Murmansk Region, contain poor ores, but the reserves there are bigger than those of all the deposits on the Kola Peninsula put together. The ores of the Kostomuksha deposit are easily concentrated by magnetic separation and provide concentrates containing from 60 to 62 per cent of iron, the production cost being somewhat lower than that of the ores from the Kola Peninsula. Furthermore, the Kostomuksha deposit is located nearer (by 350 km.) the Cherepovets Iron and Steel Works.

The Pudozh deposit of titanium-magnetite iron ores has been discovered in the western part of the Karelian ASSR. However, it will be rational to build an iron and steel works there only at some future date, when the problem of obtaining cheap electric power in the north-western part of the European North is finally resolved.

The utilisation of the large reserves of cyanite raw materials for the refractory and aluminium industry will promote the industrial development of the eastern part of the Kola Peninsula. The known Keiv cyanite deposits are many hundred times bigger than the total known reserves of sillimanite raw materials in the world—sillimanite and cyanite in India, andalusite and cyanite in the USA, and the sillimanite in Australia.

The known reserves of the Chervurt cyanite deposits in the area of the Keiv hills are greater than the reserves of andalusite found in the biggest deposits in the USSR— the Semiz-Bugu in Kazakhstan—and many times greater than the country's total reserves of all other sillimanite raw material.

The Keiv cyanites are also the best in the USSR as regards the content of sillimanite minerals in the ore: the average content of cyanite in the Chervurt ores is twice as high as the content of andalusite in the Semiz-Bugu ores, and of cyanite in the Khizovara deposits. Their utilisation will make it possible greatly to increase the amount of raw materials for the production of aluminium and high-quality refractories. Technico-economic studies have shown that the electro-thermal method of producing aluminium directly from cyanite concentrates, elaborated by Soviet scientists, is most effective. However, since the production of aluminium from cyanites is very power-intensive, their utilisation depends on the availability of cheap power.

The Karelian ASSR is situated in the eastern part of the Finno-Scandinavian (Baltic) crystalline shield, consisting mainly of ancient metamorphic rocks. The republic has a wealth of building materials (granite, diabase, quartzite, sandstone, etc.), vast reserves of pegmatite, commercial reserves of mica, iron ore and other minerals.

The extraction of granite, diabases, marble, quartzite and sandstone is concentrated on the shores of lakes Onega and Ladoga. These building materials are supplied to Leningrad and other big centres. Mica is extracted in the northern part of Karelia. The republic supplies feldspars and quartzites to many porcelain factories all over the country.

The northern part of Karelia resembles the Kola Peninsula as regards geological structure. It is therefore extremely likely that many useful minerals will be discovered there, and that this will have a considerable effect on the republic's future economic development.

Fishing

Murmansk Region supplies about 20 per cent of the total Soviet fish catch. The well-equipped fishing port of Murmansk is one of the biggest in the world. Murmansk Region has a large trawler fleet and several big fish-processing enterprises. Atlantic herring is caught in the fishing grounds extending from the Norwegian coast to Jan Mayen Island, and the Atlantic Ocean is also fished. The big trawlers of the Murmansk fishing fleet take on enough fuel and fresh water to stay at sea for many days and are equipped to process fish on board, which makes them very effective economically.

Fuel and Electricity

If the vast mineral and timber resources of the area are to be fully utilised on a commercial scale considerable efforts must be made to provide cheap fuel and electric power. The fuel used in Murmansk Region and the Karelian ASSR costs 50 per cent more than it does in other parts of the European USSR. Coal and heavy oil have to be delivered from points 1,500-2,000 km. away. The main source of power is the water power of the local rivers, which can supply 31,000 million kwh. a year, and which are largely being utilised already. Multi- and single-stage hydroelectric power stations have been built on the Niva, Paz, Tuloma, Vyg, Suma, Kem and other rivers. The power they produce is more expensive than that produced by the big hydroelectric stations in other regions, but costs several times less than the power supplied by the local thermal power stations, which have to work on coal from the distant Pechora and Donets coalfields.

A single power grid (Kolenergo) has been created in the Kola Peninsula, while three separate power grids—the South Karelian, linked with the Leningrad grid, the Central Karelian and the Ladoga—are functioning in the Karelian ASSR.

Prospects are now good for supplying the area with somewhat cheaper fuel and electric power. Firstly, gas from the Vuktyl deposit in the Komi ASSR will be supplied to Petrozavodsk, a large fuel and power consumer. Secondly, in view of a great increase in oil production in the Ukhta region and the building of oil refineries in the North-West Economic Region, Murmansk Region and Karelia will receive heavy oil at less than half the cost of Pechora coal. Thirdly, atomic power stations are to be built. The first stage of an atomic power station has been built in Murmansk Region and the second stage is now under construction according to the decisions of the 24th CPSU Congress. Improvements in atomic power station technology makes it possible to lower the cost of the power produced, making such plants economical in all regions where expensive fuel is used, including Murmansk Region and Karelia. Finally, the utilisation of tidal energy is also becoming a reality. The total reserves of such energy on the northern coast of the Kola Peninsula and Mezen Guba are estimated at 40,000 million kwh. A pilot plant has been built at Kislaya Guba in Murmansk Region and several similar stations are projected for the northern coast. The large Belomorsk hydroelectric power station, to be constructed at Mezen Guba, is to produce 3,500 million kwh. a year, and some of that power could be transmitted to Murmansk Region. Tidal power stations produce electric power very irregularly, so that they are only an economic proposition where they can be linked up in a single grid with hydro- and thermal-power stations. This is feasible in Murmansk Region.

Without the next few years all the power grids of Murmansk Region and the Karelian ASSR will be interlinked and connected with the power system of the entire European USSR, making electric supplies much more reliable.

All this offers a very promising prospect as regards the solution of the fuel and power problem in the North-West of the Soviet Union's European North.

Agriculture and Traditional Occupations

In view of the unfavourable soil and climatic conditions, the shortage of manpower (aggravated by the growth of industry) and the high costs involved, agriculture is ancillary in this area. Its purpose is to satisfy the population's requirements for such perishable products as fresh milk, vegetables and potatoes. The rapid growth of the urban population encourages the development of agriculture within economically rational limits. The bulk of the agricultural produce, as well as concentrated cattle fodder, is brought by railway from other parts of the country located in more favourable climatic zones, where the cost of the production of grain and other produce is very much lower.

Only about 2 per cent of the total area is agricultural land. In Murmansk Region about 3 per cent of the gainfully employed population is engaged in agriculture, in the Karelian ASSR about 8 per cent. Dairy and meat cattle-breeding is the leading branch. In Murmansk Region and the northern districts of Karelia the cattle is table-nursed practically all year round. The cattle, especially in Murmansk Region, is of an improved breed, and provides the highest milk yields in the country. Pig-breeding is developed, and the sheep and goat herds are big. Fodder crops hold a leading place in the agricultural produce. In the state farms and farms run by industrial enterprises of Murmansk Region that are located in the zone gravitating towards the railway, potatoes and vegetables are grown in open and hothouse conditions.

In Karelia agriculture is developed mainly in the southern part of the republic. The soddy-podzolic and peat-boggy soils require improvement and considerable amelioration work is being carried on in an area exceeding 100,000 ha. In addition to fodder and grain crops, potatoes and vegetables are cultivated, notably cabbages.

Since the arable lands are extremely scattered throughout the area, even in southern Karelia, mechanical equipment can only be used on a limited scale and much of the work has to be done by hand.

There are good prospects for hothouse cultivation in both Karelia and Murmansk Region. The steam recuperated from thermal power stations and the boiler rooms of large industrial enterprises can be used for heating the greenhouses.

Reindeer-breeding, carried on by the native population— the Saami, Nentsi and Komi—is developed in the eastern part of Murmansk Region. There are over 80,000 head of reindeer there and they provide a high and steady income. A large part of the reindeer meat is supplied to the towns.

Fur-farming, as well as hunting and trapping, are important. The waste from fishing, hunting and trapping is ideal as fodder for the fur-farms. There are dozens of fur-farms and special state farms in Karelia and Murmansk Region breeding mink, silver fox and other fur-bearing animals. A large share of the output of these farms is exported. Squirrels, muskrat and other fur-bearing animals are hunted in the Karelian forests.

Transportation

The transport network is the most developed in the European North. There are some 3,000 km. of railways, 2,000 km. of roads, thousands of kilometres of water routes—sea (the Barents and White seas), lake (the Onega, Ladoga and the numerous other lakes, of which there are 43,000 in Karelia) and inland waterways (the White Sea-Baltic Canal and the rivers).

The Murmansk Railway traverses the Karelian ASSR and Murmansk Region from south to north, and has branches leading to mines, industrial towns and workers' settlements. Most important of these are the railway from Kola to Pechenga and Nikel, the nickel mining districts in the west of the Kola Peninsula, and the line from Olenya to

Monchegorsk (centre of the nickel industry), Apatity to Kirovsk (centre of the apatite industry).

Of great importance to the further economic development of the Karelian ASSR is the West Karelian Railway, running from the Murmansk trunk line to Suoyarvi, and thence northward to Yushkozero. It is to be continued to Sofporog on the shore of Lake Topozero, which is already linked to the Murmansk line at Loukhi, so that eventually the West Karelian Railway will form a ring embracing the most populated part of the republic. The new railway also opens up prospects for the intensive exploitation of the timber resources of western Karelia, and gives access to the big Kostomuksha iron ore deposits.

There are a large number of relatively short motor roads connecting various populated centres with the Murmansk trunk line and also between many towns and settlements. The freight traffic along these roads is very heavy, twice as heavy as that on the roads of industrial Leningrad Region.

The seaport of Murmansk, ice-free throughout the year, is one of the leading seaports of the USSR. The export cargoes it handles include many items from Karelia and Murmansk Region—timber, apatite concentrate, iron ore and fish products.

Freight traffic is also heavy on the inland waterways. In Karelia the waterways handle only 50 per cent less traffic than the railways. A large goods traffic passes from north to south along the White Sea-Baltic Canal, mainly timber, iron ore, apatite concentrates, building stone, with manufactured goods, foodstuffs and other cargoes going in the other direction.

The extensive transport network and the convenient geographic position favours the further development of the productive forces in the North-West.

* * *

Thus, the North-West of the northern part of the European USSR has reached a considerable level of development and has very promising prospects for further growth. The prospects are particularly favourable in Murmansk Region, where the gigantic mineral deposits are to be tapped, and where the fuel and power problem is being solved by using the local water-power resources to the full, harnessing tidal energy, supplying relatively cheap electric power from other regions and building atomic power stations. The big fishing industry and the fact that various auxiliary branches, services and amenities have been provided for the population also promote development.

The rapid growth of the population in that essentially inhospitable region raises the question of setting up "supply bases" in the southern part of Karelia, where much more favourable natural conditions prevail. Such supply bases could be used to promote the development of the leading economic branches of the Kola Peninsula. Prefabricated building elements and parts, produced at these bases by industrial methods, could be delivered by railway to building sites in Murmansk Region, and all major overhauls of machinery and equipment could also be carried out there.

Murmansk Region has many industrial centres and new ones are springing up all the time. Most important are:

The town of Murmansk, population 296,000 in 1968— 350,000 (40 per cent of the total for the region) including the urban settlements around it (Murmashi, Kola, etc.). Murmansk is the administrative centre of the region, and one of the country's leading ice-free seaports, handling a large share of the Soviet Union's foreign trade. It is also an industrial centre, with big fish-canning plants, shipyards and metal-working plants (geared to sea transport and the fishing industry), large electric power plants (Murmashi), and light and food industries. The Murmansk economy is to be technically reconstructed shortly, and this will raise the port's capacity, increase the output and improve the quality of the fish products, and provide more and better services and amenities for the population.

Kirovsk and Apatity, centre of apatite-nepheline mining and the country's main base for the production of apatite concentrate. A double-magnesium superphosphate factory is to be built here, as well as various enterprises to cater for the developing industry and the steadily increasing population. The Kola branch of the USSR Academy of Sciences is situated in Apatity.

Monchegorsk, centre of the processing of complex copper-nickel ores, the production of nickel and copper, involving the utilisation of some other valuable components.

The Pechenga industrial centre which includes the town of Zapolyarny and the urban settlements of Nikel, Pechenga and Gorny situated in the vicinity of copper and nickel deposits. The town of Zapolyarny has an ore-dressing plant, and a workshop for the production of sulphuric acid from the waste gases of the nickel factories is under construction there. The centre is supplied with power from the cascade of hydroelectric power plants on the Paz River.

The Olenegorsk industrial centre, which includes the iron ore combine and the settlements near the iron ore deposits. A big mechanical repair plant under construction in Olenegorsk will cater for the needs of a cluster of industrial centres (Kirovsk, Apatity, Monchegorsk, Olenegorsk and others).

The Yena-Kovdor industrial centre (the town of Kovdor and Yena settlement), which includes the iron ore-dressing plant in Kovdor and the mica mines in Yena, where valuable Muscovite mica is extracted. The further development of this centre is linked with the all-round utilisation of iron ores containing apatite, rare elements and other components, and also with the exploitation in the district of the big deposits of amber mica and vermiculite, which are extremely valuable minerals.

The Kandalaksha industrial centre (the town of Kandalaksha and the settlements of Nivsky and Zelenoborsky)which has a small aluminium plant powered from a cascade of hydroelectric power stations on the Niva River. It also has sawmills and is a centre for processing the timber from the forests of southern Murmansk Region. The food and light industry enterprises supply other towns in Murmansk Region.

Within the next 10 to 15 years a number of new industrial centres will spring up in Murmansk Region: the Afrikanda centre—to work the titanium-magnetite deposits, the big Keiv centre, to utilise the practically inexhaustible cyanite reserves in the eastern part of the Kola Peninsula and the Lovozero centre, to tap the rare metals and other minerals found in the Lovozero tundra.

As more and more of its huge natural resources are exploited, Murmansk Region will be of ever greater importance to the Soviet economy.

The development of the Karelian ASSR depends largely on the rational utilisation of its timber resources. The task now is to make fuller and more extensive use of this valuable raw material. More rational utilisation of timber and higher labour productivity are to increase production in terms of value many times over, despite the fact that the volume of timber felled is to be reduced. The republic will supply more machinery for the timber and wood-processing industry, and some of its minerals—iron ore, mica, pegmatite, marble, etc.—will be used on a larger scale. Extensive geological prospecting is to be launched in the northern part of Karelia, which resembles the Kola Peninsula as regards its geological structure. The economic structure of the Karelian ASSR may change if a high concentration of valuable minerals is discovered there. The republic will play a more important role as the nearest supply base for the industrial Murmansk Region.

The main industrial centres in the Karelian ASSR are:

Petrozavodsk, with a population of 185,000, the administrative and chief industrial centre of the republic. It is the seat of the Onega lumber tractor plant, which is delivering tractors for the entire timber industry of the European North and also to other regions. Building is nearing completion of a big paper-making machinery factory, which will supply equipment for the pulp-and-paper industry not only of the European North, but also of other well-forested regions. There are several small factories for the repair of port equipment, lorries and equipment for the timber industry, light and food industries and a mica factory.

Kondopoga, some 37 km. from Petrozavodsk, a centre of the timber-processing industry, with a big pulp-and-paper combine supplied by a number of lumbering enterprises.

Segezha, including the town of Segezha and the settlement of Nadvoitsy. The former has a pulp-and-paper mill, the latter, an aluminium plant. These two industrial centres lie very close to each other, and share a number of auxiliary enterprises.

Belomorsk, with the town of Belomorsk and the settlements of Letnerechensky and Sosnovets which specialise in forestry and wood-working, as well as in the processing of fish and sea mammals.

An industrial centre is to be set up shortly at Kostomuksha (iron ore deposits), and the Pudozh centre (titanium-magnetite ores) is to be built up at a somewhat later date.

2. The North-East

General

This area comprises Arkhangelsk Region and the Komi ASSR, linked by two railways—the Northern Railway passing through Vologda to Arkhangelsk, and the Pechora Railway, running from Kotlas in a north-easterly direction to Vorkuta and Khalmer-Yu.

The area lies between the eastern edge of the Baltic crystalline shield and the Ural Mountains and occupies an extensive plain, dissected by broad depressions through which flow the main rivers of the European North—the Northern Dvina, Pechora, Mezen and their tributaries. The watersheds are flat and very marshy. A wide tundra belt extends across the north. In the central part of the lowland rises the relatively low, ancient and heavily eroded Timan ridge, forming the watershed between the Pechora, Mezen and Vychegda rivers.

The moderating influence of air streams from the Atlantic is much less than in the Kola Peninsula, and decreases towards the north-east and south. The climate is thus increasingly continental towards the south and east, and the winters there are long, cold and windy.

The mean January temperature is minus 13°C in Arkhangelsk Region and drops to 19-21°C in Pechora and the foothills of the Ural Mountains. The mean July temperature is higher towards the south, and reaches plus 17°-18°C in the southernmost districts. Precipitation is 500-550 mm. a year in the south, decreasing towards the north-east to 250-300 mm. The vegetation period lasts on an average from 115 to 170 days. Late spring and early autumn frosts, having an adverse effect on agriculture, are a feature of the whole area.

Though Arkhangelsk Region and the Komi ASSR have many features in common, there are also considerable differences between them, especially as regards natural resources, economic specialisation and geographical transport situation.

At the present time timber is the only widely utilised natural resource in Arkhangelsk Region, its specialisation in the inter-regional division of labour. In addition to the timber industry, the Komi ASSR specialises also in mining—

coal-mining in the Pechora coal basin and the extraction of oil and gas in the Ukhta district. The mining industry of Arkhangelsk Region will greatly develop in future, for a number of useful minerals have been discovered there. The exploitation of the big North Onega bauxite deposits has begun by decision of the 24th Congress.

As regards its geographical transport situation Arkhangelsk Region holds an intermediate position between the North-West of the European North and the Komi ASSR. Like the North-West, it is closely linked with the White Sea basin into which the Northern Dvina and Onega rivers flow. The Northern Railway extends to the port of Arkhangelsk, and the Obozerskoye-Belomorsk railway links the Northern and the Murmansk trunk lines and forms an additional egress to the ice-free port of Murmansk through Arkhangelsk Region.

On the other side, the right-bank tributaries of the Northern Dvina (the Vychegda and other rivers) penetrate far to the east, to the Komi ASSR. The Pechora and Mezen rivers, their lower reaches flowing through Arkhangelsk Region, in their central and upper reaches cross the least developed part of the Komi ASSR. The Pechora Railway runs right across the Komi ASSR from the south-west to the north-east linking it with the Northern Dvina basin. Coal from Pechora is brought by railway to Kotlas whence it is shipped by river to Arkhangelsk.

Arkhangelsk Region always enjoyed a more favourable geographic transport situation than the Komi ASSR. At the end of the 19th century there was already a railway linking Arkhangelsk with the central industrialised parts of the country, while to the north and west there is the sea. The Komi ASSR, on the other hand, had no railways till 1942, when the Pechora Railway was opened, and the Vychegda River (during the navigational season) was the only transport artery linking the republic with Kotlas—the nearest point on the railway. The Pechora does not provide a convenient egress to the sea because of the shallow bar in the mouth of the river and the short duration of the navigational season.

The above differences in the geographic-transport conditions greatly affected the development of the productive forces in those regions in pre-revolutionary times and in the first stages of their industrial development during the Soviet period. The development of forestry in Arkhangelsk Region was begun soon after the establishment of Soviet power, and its coastal position led to the development of big shipyards (Arkhangelsk, Onega, etc.).

Numerous repair and metal-working factories were set up to serve the timber industry, agriculture, road and river transport. On the whole the economy of Arkhangelsk Region reached a considerable level of development, especially in the zone adjacent to the railway and along the banks of the Northern Dvina. The lands to the east and north-east of the Northern Dvina remain undeveloped. There are huge, and as yet virtually untapped forests, in the basins of the Mezen, Pinega and lower Pechora rivers. Detailed geological prospecting is needed in these places for there are indications of large oil and gas deposits.

The southern part of the Komi ASSR has long been settled, the traditional occupations being agriculture, tar-distilling and a certain amount of hunting and fishing. In Soviet times forestry was begun in the parts of the Vychegda and Lu-za river basins lying closest to communications and centres of population. The rich forests in the eastern and northern parts of the republic are still practically untouched. Later the oil deposits in the Ukhta district were tapped, and after the building of the railway, coal-mining was developed in the Pechora basin. The industrial development of the north-eastern part is carried on by setting up separate industrial nuclei (oases) for the exploitation of the coal, oil, gas and timber resources. Some of them, like Vorkuta and Ukhta, have become major centres, others are still in an embryonic stage. On the whole, however, the indus-trialisation of the part gravitating towards the Pechora Railway is proceeding apace.

The wealth and diversity of natural resources much needed by the country's economy opens up prospects of extensive industrial development to the Komi ASSR.

Forestry

Arkhangelsk Region and the Komi ASSR are among the most densely forested regions of the European USSR. Even though more and more timber is being cut every year, there are still vast areas which have hardly been touched, partic-

The Komi ASSR. Building of the Syktyvkar timber-processing combine

Shops of the new cardboard factory of the Arkhangelsk paper-and-pulp combine

A depatrment of the co-operative fur-farm in Udor, Komi ASSR

Syktyvkar. The Komi branch of the USSR Academy of Sciences

The first section of the Messoyakha-Norilsk gas pipeline

The new face of the ancient town of Surgut, now the centre of the oil industry in the middle reaches of the Ob

A new oil well gushes forth in the Ob North

A road being built to the new wells in the West Siberian Lowland

ularly in the basins of the Mezen, Pechora and Pinega rivers. While timber felling in the European USSR is to be reduced, forestry is going to be of increasing importance in these areas. This is promoted by the rapid development there of the pulp-and-paper and wood-chemical industries, hitherto mainly developed in Arkhangelsk Region.

Arkhangelsk is the biggest of the old wood-processing centres, and has dozens of enterprises with a capacity of about 7.5 million cu.m. of timber a year. The raw timber is sent to Arkhangelsk by the Northern Railway, or by floating it down the Northern Dvina and its tributaries. Much of the timber is floated down the Vychegda, Sukhona, Yug, Vaga and Kokshenga rivers.

Arkhangelsk's wood-processing industry, using shorts and the waste from the many sawmills, is steadily growing in importance. At present the Arkhangelsk and Solombal pulp-and-paper mills are being reconstructed and expanded, wood-chemical enterprises are under construction, and also factories for the production of chipboard, etc.

Among the other centres of the timber-processing industry in Arkhangelsk Region mention should be made of Kotlas, where the pulp-and-paper industry is concentrated, and of the Onega and Mezen centres. A number of saw mills and other timber-processing enterprises have been set up along the railway and in the mouths of the rivers.

A large proportion of the timber goes to Kaliningrad Region to supply the pulp-and-paper mill there, to the coal-mining regions of the South and the Centre (support timber), and to the country's railways (sleepers, sawn timber, etc.) and part of the processed timber is exported.

The timber reserves of the Komi ASSR exceed those of Arkhangelsk Region. However, the productivity of the forests is much lower. In the extensive zone bordering on the tundra forests grow only on the watersheds, and the trees are predominantly low. As in Arkhangelsk Region, the Komi timber reserves consist mainly of coniferous species of a mature and overmature age.

In 1967 a total of 19.1 million cu.m. was felled, which is three times more than in 1940. Cutting was concentrated mainly in the basins of the Vychegda and Luza rivers. A large amount of timber was procured also in the Pechora River basin, where the timber is used mainly for local needs, to satisfy the requirements of the building and coal-mining industries. Procurements in the Mezen River basin are small because various obstacles prevent floating the timber, there are no roads, and navigation is difficult in the mouth of the river.

The wood-processing industry is far less developed than in Arkhangelsk Region, and has been built up mainly during the past 20 to 25 years. Only 20 per cent of the timber is processed locally, and 60 per cent is shipped out of the republic unprocessed (round timber). The industry is to be developed and made more efficient in the near future.

Syktyvkar, the capital of the Komi ASSR, has become a major new timber-processing centre. One of the biggest timber combines in the USSR became operational there in 1969: when it reaches its rated output it will process about 3 million cu.m. of timber a year, making full use of the raw material and producing pulp, paper, plywood, cardboard, hydrolysis products, etc.

The combine will process timber of inferior quality, wood, waste from saw mills and wood-working enterprises, and waste of sulphide-pulp enterprises. The sawing of high-quality timber will be concentrated at Syktyvkar.

A number of existing timber-processing centres will be expanded, and new centres will be set up in Ust-Kuloma, Troitsko-Pechorskoye, to which a railway is being built, and in other areas with huge timber reserves.

Minerals

The heterogeneous geological structure of the area explains the diversity of economic minerals found there. Professor A. A. Chernov, a prominent geologist, divides them into four geological structural units, with corresponding minerals: 1) the Pechora Urals with its spurs, embracing the western slope of the Near-Polar and Polar Urals, and the territory between the Urals and the Timan Ridge, 2) the Novaya Zemlya bulge, including the Pai-Khoi range and the islands of Vaigach and Novaya Zemlya, 3) the Timan Ridge, and 4) the northern part of the Russian Platform. Among the above structural units the Pechora Urals and the Timan Ridge are richest in minerals.

The coal deposits in the Pechora basin, the biggest in the European USSR, are Lower Permian deposits. The geological coal reserves in it exceed 300,000 million tons, i.e., they are twice as large as those of the Donets coalfields. There are also huge reserves of furnace and coking coals in the Pechora basin. In fact, it contains all the kinds of coal necessary to obtain furnace charges for the production of high-quality coke.

Polymetallic ore deposits are found in a broad band extending along the Novaya Zemlya bulge. Non-ferrous metal deposits have been found in the Pai-Khoi and on the islands of Vaigach and Novaya Zemlya, but with the exception of a few deposits on Vaigach none of them are of commercial significance. But fluorite deposits have been discovered on the Amderma River.

The Timan Ridge is an ancient and strongly eroded mountainous land. Extensive oil- and gas-bearing areas are found in the Devon deposits of the southern part of the Timan Ridge and the Pechora basin. The entire area from the Timan Ridge to the western spurs of the Urals forms the very promising Timano-Pechora oil-bearing province. In recent years the huge Vuktyl natural gas deposit has been discovered and is already worked there. Oil has been found on the Usa.

The northern part of the Russian Platform is a region where the Baltic shield is relatively deeply immersed and overlaid with paleozoic sedimentary deposits. Gypsum and rock salt deposits have been discovered in the Kotlas district, and combustible shales and phosphorites have been found in the south-east.

The carboniferous and Permian deposits contain an abundance of limestone and dolomites, of which there are outcrops in many places on the banks of the Northern Dvina, Onega, Sukhona, Pinega, Vychegda, in the vicinity of the Northern Railway, etc. The diversity of minerals makes it possible to use them not only as building materials, but also as industrial raw materials (e.g., for the production of cellulose and glass, in agriculture). Raw materials for the cement industry have been found on the Northern Dvina. Big bauxite deposits have recently been discovered in the Onega basin. It is believed that there are oil deposits in the northern part of the Russian Platform. Raw materials for the production of building materials—brick clay, cobblestone, sand (including some suitable for glass-making) are found throughout this north-east area.

In evaluating the minerals in that region from the point of view of their industrial utilisation, the following should be noted:

1. Most important of the economic minerals being extracted at present is coal in the Pechora coalfields.

2. The discovery of oil and gas in the Timano-Pechora province, the tapping of which will be of great importance for the whole of the European USSR, especially for the North-West and Centre economic regions, holds out the greatest prospects.

3. The big titanium and bauxite deposits are also of great importance. The geological structure of the Pechora Urals, the Novaya Zemlya bulge and the Timan Ridge suggests that non-ferrous and rare metals are likely to be found there.

4. Raw materials for the production of building materials are found practically throughout the North-East area, and the limestones and dolomites on the Northern Dvina can become a base for a huge cement industry, which will facilitate the setting-up on the spot of construction bases.

Fuel

The Komi ASSR has over 95 per cent of all the potential fuel reserves of the North-East Economic Region, or about 50 per cent of the fuel reserves of the European USSR. However, the coal mined in the republic is more expensive than that from the Donets coalfields by the time it reaches the main consumers (Leningrad, Murmansk Region, etc.). The same applies to the oil products extracted in the Ukhta district. This discourages the utilisation of the vast mineral and raw material resources of the North-East.

It has now become possible to extract more fuel more cheaply in the Komi ASSR, and to use it to greater advantage in the economy of many regions of the European USSR.

Let us look at the prospects for a rational utilisation of the huge fuel resources of the North-East.

The Pechora coalfields occupy an enormous area of almost 130,000 sq.km. Coal of different kinds and varying quality is found there. Its geological reserves exceed 300,000 million tons, and about 50 per cent of the known reserves consist of coking coal. Rich coal, used in the iron and steel industry, makes up the largest share (40 per cent), and represents the largest worked deposits in the USSR. At present rich coal mined chiefly in the Vorkuta district accounts for two-thirds of the Pechora output.

Mining in the Pechora coalfields was intensified following the building of the Pechora Railway during the Second World War, when the Donets coalfields—the main fuel base of the European USSR—were in German hands. Pechora coal played an important role also in the initial post-war period, when the Donets basin was being rehabilitated. In subsequent years output stabilised at the level of 17-18 million tons a year. Recently, however, some new factors are contributing to the wider and economically more advantageous utilisation of the Pechora coal, especially coking coal.

The development of the Kursk Magnetic Anomaly, the largest iron ore deposit in the country, raised the demand for coking coals in the central regions of the European USSR. Estimates and experience of using Pechora coals at the Cherepovets Iron and Steel Works demonstrated that even at their present high cost it is economically expedient to supply them to the iron and steel works in the central regions of the European USSR. The Pechora coking coals have an advantage over the coal from the Donets coalfields in that their sulphur content is less than one-third that of the latter, enabling higher metal yields to be obtained from blast furnaces. This means that the expenditure on coke per ton of smelted metal is lower when Pechora coal is used.

Moreover, new coking coal deposits have recently been discovered in the Vorkuta district, which can be mined with modern equipment at practically half the former cost. The most important of these is the Vorgashor deposit, where the seams are conveniently situated and several metres thick so that it is possible to extract 3 to 4 million tons a year. As a result, the initial capital investment and cost of mining per ton is reduced by 33-50 per cent. Estimates have shown that it is more economical to sink mines at Vorgashor than to sink very deep mines in the Donets coalfields. The transportation of coal will become much cheaper as a result of the reconstruction of the Pechora Railway and its transfer to diesel traction, now in progress, and the planned electrification will eventually make the utilisa-

117

tion of the Pechora coking coal in the central regions even more rational.

The growth in the production of coking coal in the Pechora basin will raise the effectiveness of the utilisation of the big fixed industrial assets in that region.

In addition to coking coal, some furnace coal is mined in the Pechora basin for the local needs of the Komi ASSR.

The oil and gas industry, based on the deposits of the Timano-Pechora oil- and gas-bearing province, holds out major development prospects.

The volume of the oil and gas produced here is still relatively small. Until recently the heavy oil, extracted by the mine method, accounted for a large share of the yield. These are the only oil mines in the country. Heavy oil is very viscous and resinous, contains a large percentage of sulphur, and has a low kerosene and ligroin content, and no gasoline fractions. The Ukhta oil refinery makes tractor kerosene, bitumen, various kinds of marine diesel and other valuable and frost-resistant oils used in many parts of the USSR.

Low-density oil is extracted at the West Tebuk, Chibyu, Voi-Vozh, Nibel and other deposits. This oil has a considerable content of gasoline, kerosene and ligroin fractions, a small sulphur and paraffin content. The Ukhta refinery produces gasoline and kerosene, diesel oil and fuel oil from light oil. The oil products are used mainly in the European North.

Natural gas is produced at the Vuktyl deposit and at many smaller deposits in the basins of the Lower Omra, Nyamed and Sed-Yola rivers.

New factors favour an enormous increase in oil and gas production there in the near future. Even though a detailed survey is yet to be undertaken, it is possible to outline the borders of the Timano-Pechora oil- and gas-bearing province, embracing an area of 600,000 sq. km. If geological forecasts prove true, the Komi ASSR will become one of the most important bases for cheap fuel for the country's northwestern, central and western regions. The forecast gas reserves amount to several trillion cubic metres. Proof of the correctness of these favourable forecasts is the discovery of the Vuktyl deposit of condensed gas, estimated to contain 650,000 million cu.m. This exceeds the reserves of the famous Gazli deposits in Central Asia from which gas is supplied to Moscow by 3,000-km.-long pipeline. The development of the Vuktyl deposit has already begun. The building of the 1,400-km.-long Vuktyl-Ukhta-Cherepovets-Torzhok pipeline was completed in 1969, and it now conducts gas to the north-western regions via pipes with a diameter of 1.22 m. Two more large-diameter pipelines will be built and gas deliveries will reach thousands of millions of cubic metres a year. The Vuktyl-Ukhta-Cherepovets-Torzhok pipeline is the first section of the Siyaniye Severa (Northern Lights) pipeline, running from the northern districts of Tyumen Region to the south-west, which will have branches delivering cheap fuel to Arkhangelsk and Petrozavodsk. Thus, practically all the northern regions of the European USSR will be supplied with gas.

By 1970 oil production in the Komi ASSR was ten times the 1958 figure. Since production is to increase rapidly and there are not enough local facilities to process it, an oil pipeline will be built from Ukhta to the central regions of the European USSR.

The Timano-Pechora oil-bearing province, which is an extension to the north of the Ural-Volga oil- and gas-bearing region—the main oil and gas base of the USSR—is to be thoroughly prospected within the next few years, and may become a major fuel source for the European USSR.

The chemical industry is as yet weakly developed in the North-East, but the conditions are favourable for its development. Since it is linked with the processing of timber, the pulp-and-paper and wood-chemical industries will be developed first. The question of setting up a chemical industry on the basis of oil and natural gas, titanium, rock salt, etc., is under consideration.

The deposits of chlorine, hydrocarbon and metal ore are situated favourably in relation to each other in the Komi ASSR. A big rock salt deposit has been discovered near the village of Seregovo. In the next few years a factory producing annually 100,000 tons of table salt will be built there. However, the basic trend is to use the deposit for the production of chlorine and caustic soda. Chlorine is used as a bleaching agent in the pulp-and-paper industry. It is also expedient to organise the production there of chlorine-organic synthesis products, which can be done where raw materials, water resources and cheap power are readily available. The production of synthetic resins will also be organised on a considerable scale.

The Komi ASSR will also become a supplier of pigments, to be obtained using titanium dioxide, the biggest deposits of which are near the Yarega heavy oil deposits. According to estimates, the titanium concentrates from the Komi ASSR will cost less than titanium concentrates of the same quality coming from other deposits.

The low-calory coal with a high ash content found in the Inta deposit is also a major source of chemical raw material. It can be used for the production of nitrogen ferti- lisers, as a raw material for plastics, for gasoline with a high octane number, and for a number of other products. Raw materials for potash fertilisers are also found in the Komi ASSR.

Thus, wide prospects are opening up in the North-East area of the European North for the development of the timber, wood-processing, chemical and fuel industries, involving the more extensive utilisation of coking and furnace coal from the Pechora basin, of the resources of oil and gas, bauxites and titanium. This will also promote the development of the auxiliary enterprises whose purpose is to secure the continuous operation of the branches in which the region is specialising, and satisfy the needs of the population; among the latter are the building materials factories and the construction industry, workshops for the repair of machinery, lorries, sea and river vessels, and light and food industry enterprises.

Agriculture and Traditional Occupations

Agriculture is more developed in the North-East of the European North than it is in the North-West, even though only 1.5 per cent of the total area is cultivated. Agriculture is carried on mainly on suburban farms, to supply the population with potatoes, vegetables, meat and dairy products.

The sown area and number of cattle are 100 to 150 per cent bigger in Arkhangelsk Region than in the Komi ASSR. Dairy farming is the leading branch. Highly productive cattle, famed throughout the country, is bred in the Khol- mogory and Primorsky districts in Arkhangelsk Region. The local pedigree cattle farm supplies Kholmogory cattle to various collective and state farms in the European North and in many other parts of the country to improve local breeds. During the 35 years the state pedigree cattle farm has existed it has supplied over 130,000 head of pedigree cattle to over 30 regions of the USSR. The strain is constantly being improved.

On the whole, conditions do not favour crop farming in the North-East, and grain crops are grown only in southern Arkhangelsk Region and southern and central Komi ASSR. Even there, the bulk of the sown area is under fodder crops. Relatively small areas are under potatoes and vegetables, mainly in suburban farms. Some flax is grown in the extreme south-east and south-west. Agriculture is largely confined to the floodplains of the numerous rivers, on small scattered plots—on some collective farms in Arkhangelsk Region there are several hundred such plots, each only a fraction of a hectare in area. This makes mechanisation practically impossible, and puts up the expenditure of labour and time, and, hence, costs. It might seem that the abundance of meadows should provide ample fodder for the cattle. However, since most of them are very boggy or overgrown with shrubbery there is a shortage of pasture-land in many localities, and drainage and other land improvement measures have to be carried out. Grain crops, the cultivation of which requires additional labour expenditure in these parts, give small (0.6-0.7 tons per hectare) yields, and there is a tendency to reduce the areas under grain. With the growing productivity of the cattle, numbers are tending to stabilise (in 1967 there were 412,000 head of cattle, including 236,000 cows; 97,000 pigs, 203,000 sheep and goats), because most of the concentrated fodder has to be brought from other regions.

Reindeer-breeding is carried on, especially in the Nenets National Area, where they number between 150,000 and 175,000. There are herds in the tundras of the Mezen and Leshukonsk districts of Arkhangelsk Region, and over 60,000 in the northern Komi ASSR. Reindeer-breeding is a traditional occupation of the native population (the Nentsi and Komi). The herds are driven for the summer from the taiga districts of the Komi ASSR to the tundras in Nenets National Area and return for the winter. The reindeer breeders deliver over 2,000 tons of meat to the towns in Arkhangelsk Region and the Komi ASSR.

Fur-farming is an important economic branch in the North. It is closely linked with reindeer-breeding and fishing, the latter providing fodder for the fur animals. There are about a dozen fur-farms run by collective and state farms in the Nenets National Area. Near Arkhangelsk is the Shirshinsk state fur-farm, and many collective and state farms in the Komi ASSR also run fur-farms. Hunting is also widespread.

The Kama-Vychegda-Pechora Project

The idea of linking the Pechora, Vychegda and Kama rivers to create a single waterway connecting the European North with the Volga basin was advanced a long time ago. The North-Yekaterininsky Canal was built for that purpose in the first quarter of the eighteenth century. Later, with the development of more convenient North-South road connections, the canal fell into disuse, and was closed in 1838. The idea of linking the three rivers was put forward again in Soviet times, in the early thirties, in connection with the shallowing of the Caspian Sea. It was proposed to direct the excess waters of the northern rivers to the Kama and Volga basin to increase the flow to the Caspian Sea. This would also have resolved the problem of creating a waterway linking the northern rivers with the Volga basin. After the building of a cascade of hydroelectric power stations on the Kama and the Volga, the problem of the transfer of the water from the northern rivers became even more urgent, since the Caspian Sea was shallowing even quicker than before.

The Leningrad branch of the S. Y. Zhuk All-Union Design-Prospecting and Research Institute (Gidroproekt) worked out a scheme for the transfer of part of the waters from the northern rivers to the Kama and Volga basin. It provides for the building of the Ust-Voya earth dam on the Pechora near the mouth of the Shchugora River, of the Nibel-Izhma dam between the basins of the Nibel and Izhma rivers, of the Ust-Kuloma hydrocentre on the Vychegda River below the village of Ust-Kuloma and of the Upper-Kama hydrocentre on the Kama River near the town of Borovsk (see map on opposite page). As a result, the Pechora, Vychegda and Kama are to reach a common level of 125 m. and to form a 250-cu.m. water reservoir with an area of over 15,000 sq.km.

THE KAMA-VYCHEGDA-PECHORA WATERWAY

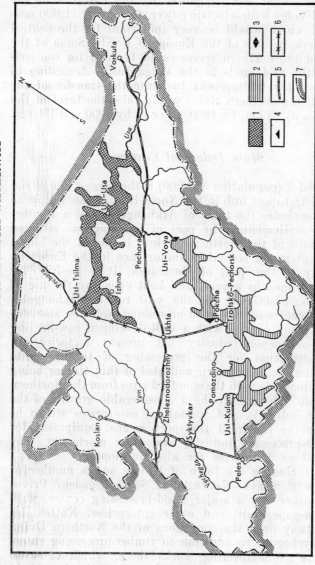

1—water reservoir of the Ust-Izhma hydroelectric power plant under construction on the Pechora;
2—Ust-Voya water reservoir on the Pechora and Ust-Kulom water reservoir on the Vychegda;
3—water catchment system and dams; 4—protective dams; 5—railways projected and under construction; 6—high-tension transmission lines from the Ust-Izhma hydroelectric power plant;
7—administrative boundaries of the Komi ASSR.

The transfer of 40 cu.km. of water a year would increase the production of electric power by the cascades of the Kama and Volga hydroelectric power stations by 11,000 million kwh., which would be very important for the central and southern regions of the European USSR. Some of the water from the northern rivers could be used for the irrigation of the arid lands in the Volga basin. According to estimates of the Gidroproekt Institute the transfer of the water from the northern rivers would raise the level of the Caspian Sea by 84 cm. by 1980, 175 cm. by 2000 and 195 cm. by 2030.

Main Industrial Centres

Arkhangelsk (population 343,000) is the biggest industrial centre and transport hub in the North-East of the European North. It includes the town of Arkhangelsk and a number of nearby settlements. The port of Arkhangelsk, situated at the mouth of the Northern Dvina, is one of the oldest in the country and second in importance in the European North only to the port of Murmansk. It is ice-free for more than 8 months a year, and kept open, by the use of ice-breakers, practically all the year round. Arkhangelsk is a major centre of the wood-processing industry and also a timber export centre, with a well developed saw-milling and pulp-and-paper industry. At present factories are under construction for the processing of timber waste (1.5-2 million cu.m. a year), and also of thin timber being delivered alongside with the standard sizes from the Northern Dvina basin. There is to be a considerable growth of the ship-repair industry, and specialised enterprises are to be set up for the repair of transport means, equipment for the timber-processing industry and other machinery. The light and food industries are also developing.

Kotlas, including the town of Kotlas and a number of workers' settlements—Koryazhma, Solvychegodsk, Privodino and others—is a major wood-processing centre, with a pulp-and-paper mill and other enterprises. Kotlas lies on the railway near the confluence of the Northern Dvina and the Vychegda. In addition to timber-processing enterprises, there are engineering works there, which cater to the needs of the timber industry and the water transport. Its central location promises well for its future growth. The creation of wood-chemical industry is intended there, as is also the production of fibre building board, synthetic fibre, etc. It is also intended to develop light and food industries, employing female labour.

In the near future a new industrial centre will be built in Plesetsk, in connection with the exploitation of the Onega bauxite deposits and the nearby limestone pits.

The chief industrial centres of the Komi ASSR are:

Syktyvkar, including the town of Syktyvkar, capital of the Komi ASSR, and nearby settlements. This is an important timber-processing centre with a wood-processing combine and several big saw mills. The food and light industries are also well represented there. In the near future chemical plants will be built to utilise the salt of the Seregovo deposit. Besides, Syktyvkar may become the supply base for the development of the remote northern districts of the Komi ASSR and the Nenets National Area, especially of the big gas deposits in the Yamal National Area. Syktyvkar is an important cultural centre, with a local branch of the USSR Academy of Sciences.

Ukhta, including the town of Ukhta and a number of settlements (Yarega, Vodny, Voi-Vozh, Zapadny Tebuk and others), the centre of the Timano-Pechora oil- and gas-bearing province. In addition to the long-established specialisations of oil and gas production and oil refining, non-ferrous metallurgy (titanium) and the chemical industry are to be developed there. A large construction base is being rapidly built up here to serve the important gas-fields of the Yamalo-Nenets National Area, as well as the Ukhta centre. It is to become one of the key industrial centres of the European North.

A new industrial centre is forming in Troitsko-Pechorsk, to the south-east of Ukhta. At present it is a small village (3,500 inhabitants), but after the completion of the Sosnogorsk-Troitsko-Pechorsk railway a large forestry and timber complex will be set up there.

Favourable prerequisites exist for the formation of an industrial centre in Mikun, at the junction of the Pechora Railway and the Syktyvkar-Mikun-Koslan line. A timber-processing centre and a repair base for the timber industry and transport will be set up there. An important industrial centre will emerge in Ust-Kulom, where a hydroelectric power station and a timber complex are to be built.

Vorkuta, including the town of Vorkuta and a number of settlements near the various coal mines (Gornyatsky, Oktyabrsky, Khalmer-Yu, Severny and others), and Inta, with the town of Inta and the adjacent workers' settlements, lie in the far north-east.

Vorkuta specialises in the extraction of coking coals, and has several big repair workshops and a building industry. Inta specialises in the extraction of furnace coals. It is situated much further to the south and will expand in connection with the big thermal power stations that are to be built there.

The formation of industrial centres in the European North will continue as further progress is made in its development, especially in view of the new natural resources being discovered there all the time.

Transportation

The transport network is far less developed than in the North-West area. Two railway trunk lines pass through the North-East with a branch from the Obozero station on the Northern railway to Belomorsk linking the Northern (Arkhangelsk) railway with the Oktyabrskaya (Murmansk) railway, and another from Mikun on the Pechora railway to Syktyvkar. The Chum-Labytnangi branch, connecting the Pechora railway with the lower reaches of the Ob River is an important factor in promoting industrial development.

A number of timber-hauling railways are under construction: the Mikun-Koslan-Yertom railway through the timber stands along the upper reaches of the Mezen and Vashka rivers, and the Arkhangelsk-Karpogory railway, towards which the forests along the middle reaches of the Mezen and Vashka rivers are gravitating. The timber resources of that district will be used at Arkhangelsk. These railways will link Arkhangelsk with Syktyvkar. A branch line is being built from the Ukhta district (Sosnogorsk station) to Troitsko-Pechorsk, later to be continued to Solikamsk. This will form a direct railway link between the Komi ASSR and the industrial centres of the Urals. A railway is also planned from Syktyvkar to Fosforitnaya, which is to have a branch extending to Ust-Kulom, where a hydro-electric power station is to be built on the Vychegda

River. The branch will cut through the forests on the Vychegda.

The completion of all these railways will give the area another meridianal trunk line, linking the northern part of Arkhangelsk Region and the Komi ASSR with the main Soviet railway network.

A very important project is the building of a railway from Vorkuta to the Yugorsky Shar Strait, and the opening of a seaport there. This railway and port will make it possible considerably to increase and facilitate the export of timber from the overwooded districts of Siberia, notably from the Ob basin, and thus reduce dependence on timber from the European USSR, where resources are running short. It will also be expedient to export coking coal from the Vorkuta coal basin through the port, and, after the completion of the Troitsko-Pechorsk-Solikamsk railway, of various export commodities from the Urals too. The port can be used for the export of oil from West Siberia. With the help of a fleet of ice-breakers it will be possible to keep the port open at least ten months a year, possibly all the year round.

The railway and the port in the Yugorsky Shar Strait are expected to be completed within the next 10-15 years.

The building of pipelines was only recently begun in the European North. The Siyaniye Severa gas pipeline, which we have already mentioned, was the first. In future, as the production of oil in the Timano-Pechora oil- and gas-bearing province increases, it will become necessary to transport oil through pipelines for long distances, notably to Yaroslavl.

Water transport is also being developed. Goods traffic along the navigable rivers and through the White Sea is constantly growing, as is also the freight turnover of the port of Arkhangelsk, which, like Murmansk, is handling big foreign trade transactions. Arkhangelsk is also the main port of the Northern Sea Route.

* * *

The European North, holding out vast prospects for industrial advance, plays an increasing role in the development of the national economy of the USSR.

A rational combination of the raw material and power resources makes it possible to supply the national economy with increasing quantities of diversified products of the timber industry, with natural gas, oil, coking coals, apatites, non-ferrous metals, iron ores, etc. The European North can supply a wide range of export commodities.

The extensive industrialisation of the European North leads to increase in its economic ties and exchange of goods with the country's industrial regions further to the south, and to the gradual strengthening of economic ties between its various economic areas. This will also be promoted by the railway branches linking the meridianal trunk lines and by the large pipelines now under construction.

The prospects for the economic development of the European North warrant the conclusion that its economic level will in the next 10-15 years reach that of many of the advanced areas of traditional settlement of the USSR.

A river port is to be built on the Angara near the Ust-Ilim hydro-power plant now under construction

The Yakutsk state university

A street in Yakutsk

Yakutia. Drag at the Aldan goldfields

Nuggets

Nikita Zakharov, a veteran hunter in Yakutia, taking home his bag

Among the spurs of the Verkhoyansk range. A helicopter bringing supplies for a team of geologists

The port of Nagayevo—the gateway of Magadan Region

CHAPTER SIX

THE SIBERIAN NORTH

The Siberian North embraces the so-called Ob North, including the Yamalo-Nenets and Khanty-Mansi national areas of Tyumen Region, and also the northern districts of Omsk and Tomsk regions, forming part of the West Siberian Economic Region, and the Yenisei North, including the Evenk and Taimyr national areas, the lower reaches of the Angara, the Turukhansk and Igarka districts of Krasnoyarsk Territory and the northern districts of the Buryat ASSR, and Irkutsk and Chita regions, forming part of the East Siberian Economic Region.

The Siberian North has an area of 3.8 million sq.km. or one-sixth of the total area of the Soviet Union. It accounts for about 60 per cent of the area of the West Siberian and East Siberian economic regions, but only 4.5 per cent of their population. The population density in Northern Siberia is about one-hundredth the average for the USSR excluding the North, and one-twenty-fifth that of Southern Siberia. Much of the area is bogland, and the development of ground communications was begun only recently. All this shows that the Siberian North provides vast scope for pioneering activity.

Extending for over 2,000 kilometres in length and breadth, Northern Siberia includes the tundra, forest-tundra and taiga zones, so that natural conditions are extremely varied. The climate is harsher than in the European North, since the influence of the warm Atlantic air streams grows weaker to the east, while the ice-bound Kara Sea acts as a factor lowering the atmospheric temperature.

The climate grows more continental from the west to east which, in particular, is expressed by the growth in the absolute temperature amplitudes (the difference between the coldest and warmest months). Thus, the absolute annual amplitudes in Salekhard, Igarka and Essei (Lake Essei to the east of Igarka), which lie practically on the same latitude, are respectively 80, 94 and 100°C. The temperature drops appreciably from the south to the north. Thus, in Yeniseisk the mean annual temperature is minus 2.2°C, and in Igarka it is minus 9.3°C. The mean temperature for the coldest month (January) is minus 22°C in Yeniseisk and minus 29.6°C in Igarka. That of the warmest month (July) is plus 17.8°C and plus 14.4°C respectively. Annual precipitation in the different areas ranges from 200 to 450 mm. a year, between 70 and 85 per cent of which is in summer. The snow cover is thin and exceeds 70 cm. only in places, for the snow is dry and fine, and easily blown away by the wind. In the south the winter lasts for 6-7 months, in the north for 8-9 months. In the north the frost-free period lasts only 50-75 days, in some places (for example on Dikson Island) 30 days, while in some places there is no frost-free period (Chelyuskin Cape, Pronchishcheva Bay, etc.). The mean annual wind velocity in the coastal areas reaches 7-9 m./sec., further inland it decreases to 3-4 m./sec. Snowstorms (occurring predominantly between October and May) occur on Dikson Island 123 days, in Igarka 66 days, and in Krasnoyarsk 34 days a year.

The rivers have a moderating influence on the climate in the lateral areas. In summer the water temperature near Salekhard sometimes reaches plus 18°C. A relatively thick layer of warm water with a temperature of plus 5°-8°C forms on the large area of the sea at the mouths of the Ob and the Yenisei.

The conditions for navigation are much better in the south-western part of the Kara Sea than in the north-eastern part. Navigation from the west to the mouths of the Ob and Yenisei is possible without ice-breakers for an average of 2.5 to 3 months a year (from the second half of July to late October). The use of powerful ice-breakers extends the navigational season to 4-5 months.

The main transport arteries of this territory are the great Siberian rivers, the Ob and the Yenisei, linking it with Siberia's industrial regions, and the route through the Kara Sea, linking it with the European USSR and foreign markets. In the early fifties a branch line of the Pechora Railway (Chum-Labytnangi) was built to the lower reaches of the Ob. A 120-km.-long railway line links the industrial centre of Norilsk with the sea and river port of Dudinka on the Yenisei. In connection with the development of its natural resources, large-scale construction of railways and roads, and oil and gas pipelines has recently begun in the Ob North.

Up to the present decade the Siberian North, which is difficult of access and, hence, difficult to develop industrially, was considered a reserve zone, and it was planned to develop its economy only at some unspecified future date. Therefore, only a few industrial nuclei were created there, mainly in the north of Eastern Siberia (Norilsk, Igarka, and forestry and timber enterprises on the lower reaches of the Angara and in the Ob North). However, when a huge oil- and gas-bearing province was discovered in the north of the West Siberian Lowland, new and unique deposits of polymetallic ores were found in the Norilsk district, and the big Udokan deposit of copper in the north of Chita Region and other valuable mineral deposits were opened up in the past decade, the situation changed radically. The exploitation of the natural resources of a number of districts in the Siberian North became a priority task. In accordance with the decisions of the 23rd and 24th Congresses of the CPSU, a large national economic complex is being created there to exploit the oil, gas and timber resources. The tapping of the new polymetallic ore deposits in the Norilsk district, the building of the 4-million-kwt. Ust-Ilim hydroelectric power station on the Angara, the development of the Korshunovo iron ore deposits, etc., have become priority tasks.

In 20-30 years the northern territories of Western and Eastern Siberia will become a vast economic area with a unified transport network. However, within the next 10-15 years the development of the West and East Siberian North will differ considerably, and we therefore propose to consider them separately, as various subdivisions.

The Ob North

The Yamalo-Nenets National Area (750,300 sq. km.), in the tundra and forest-tundra zone, and the Khanty-Mansi National Area (532,100 sq. km.), situated in the taiga zone further to the south, occupy the greater part of the Ob North (90 per cent). The northern districts of Omsk and Tomsk regions are also in the taiga zone.

The Yamalo-Nenets National Area (capital Salekhard) lies in the part of the Ob North where the harshest natural conditions prevail. According to the 1970 census the population was 80,000, with a density of 0.1 per sq. km. About one-third of the population was made up of the small nationalities of the North, of whom the Nentsi and Khanty were the most numerous, and also including Selkups, Evenks and Mansi. Like the other nationalities of the North, they are unsurpassed reindeer-breeders, hunters and fishermen.

The Yamalo-Nenets National Area is one of the most important reindeer-breeding regions. There are over 360,000 reindeer, one-sixth of the total in the USSR. Reindeer-breeding provides up to 2,000 tons of meat a year. The animals are grazing all the year round and their meat costs between a fifth and a quarter that of horned cattle.

Hunting and trapping is another traditional occupation of the native population. The hunters procure fox and polar fox, ermine, mink, and muskrat. There is also fur-farming, mainly in silver fox, mink and blue fox.

Fishing and the hunting of sea mammals hold a major place in the area's economy. A profusion of fish is found in the lower reaches of the Ob River and in Ob Guba.

Because of the harsh climate there is practically no crop farming. Potatoes (up to 80 per cent of the sown area) and vegetables are grown in places. At the same time conditions favour dairy farming: there are vast water meadows providing fodder for the cattle and making it highly productive.

The area embraces the northernmost part of the West Siberian Lowland, where the main forecast reserves of natural gas are located.

The Khanty-Mansi National Area always had a bigger population than the Yamalo-Nenets Area—now about 272,000, of which 171,000 classified as urban, the density being 0.5 per 1 sq. km. Predominant among the native population are the Khanty, scattered throughout the territory, and the Mansi. There are also many old Russian settlements. The capital of the area is Khanty-Mansiisk, lying 18 km. from the mouth

of the Irtysh. The Khanty-Mansi National Area is economically more developed than the Yamalo-Nenets. In addition
to the fishing industry, the timber industry is well developed,
with production standing at over 2 million cu. m. a year.
There is an important wood-working combine at Belogorsk.
A large part of the native population is employed in the
timber industry.

The floodlands with their fertile soils can be used as pas-
tures for the dairy cattle in summer and provide hay for
the winter. Owing to the somewhat more favourable climatic conditions, crop farming is developed alongside with
dairying. Oats, wheat, rye, vegetables, potatoes and fodder
crops give satisfactory yields. Agriculture is carried
on mainly by the Russian population. There are only one-
sixth the number of reindeer in Yamalo-Nenets, but fur-
farming and hunting and trapping are developed throughout
the area.

Rich oil and gas deposits have been discovered, and the
biggest timber stands of the Ob North are concentrated
there. This opens up wide vistas for the area's industrial
advance.

The northern districts of Omsk and Tomsk regions are
in the central reaches of the Ob River. Over 10 per cent of
the area's population live in the Ob North, which has a well-
developed timber industry and agriculture. Here the Russian population is in the majority.

Formation
of the West Siberian Economic Complex

The West Siberian Lowland is the biggest inner-platform
syncline, with geological conditions favouring the accumulation of oil and gas. This has determined the prospecting trends.
The world press called the discovery of the oil- and gas-bearing province in the northern part of the West Siberian
Lowland the discovery of the century. The oil- and gas-
bearing areas embrace a territory of about 2,000,000 sq.km.,
mainly in the northern part of the lowland. The forecast
reserves of natural gas run into tens of trillions of cu.m.,
those of oil into thousands of millions of tons, greatly exceeding the reserves of the Ural-Volga oil-bearing province—
the main oil supplier in the USSR.

MINERALS AND INDUSTRIAL CENTRES IN THE OB NORTH

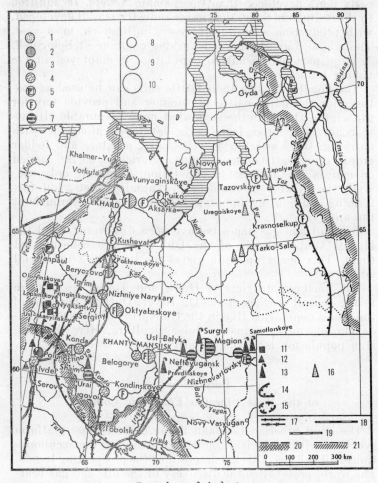

Branches of industry:
1. gas 2. iron ore mining 3. manganese ore mining 4. timber 5. mining of minerals 6. fishing 7. oil
Industrial centres:
8. small 9. medium 10. big
Minerals:
11. Coal 12. Iron ore 13. Oil 14. Boundaries of gas-bearing areas 15. Boundaries of coal-bearing areas 16. Gas

17. Oil and gas pipelines 18. Railways 19. Railways under construction 20. Southern boundary of the North 21. Boundary of the Ob North

Typical of the West Siberian oil- and gas-bearing province is the density of its reserves, which in the central reaches of the Ob exceed that of the reserves in the Ural-Volga province 3.6-fold, and that of the reserves in other oil-bearing regions of the USSR 10-15-fold. In the extreme North of Tyumen Region (the Yamalo-Nenets National Area) there is a gigantic gas-bearing region, in which the density of the gas reserves is unique. The biggest gas deposits in the USSR are found there: the Urengoisky, Zapolyarnoye, Tazovsky, Purpeiskoye, Novy Port, etc.

The oil and gas lie close to the surface, and the geological structure of the deposits makes them easy to exploit. In the West Siberian Lowland the increment of reserves per metre of descent exceeds the average for the USSR many times over. Accounting for a relatively small share of the deep probe drilling (5-7 per cent), the West Siberian province has in recent years accounted for most of the increment in the country's oil and gas reserves. Thus, in 1967 alone, geological prospecting for gas in the northern part of the lowland has doubled the known gas reserves of the USSR, bringing them up to a total of 9.2 trillion cu.m. (the biggest in the world).

The oil deposits discovered so far (over 80 of them) lie mainly in the floodlands of the central reaches of the Ob (the Khanty-Mansi National Area), in a region favourable as regards communications. It was here that geological prospecting was begun. The largest deposits are the Ust-Balyk, Megion, Sosnino-Sovietskoye. The oil in them is of a higher quality than that of the Ural-Volga province, and the yield of the wells is exceptionally high.

The Samotlor oil deposit, recently discovered near Lake Samotlor, is unique as regards its reserves and its daily yield. It is situated relatively close to Surgut in a very swampy locality.

Vast reserves of iodine-bromide geothermal waters with a commercial concentration of iodine have also been found in the West Siberian Lowland. The peat reserves in that area are estimated at 90,000-100,000 million tons. Iron ore deposits (the Bachkar and others) with geological reserves of about 100,000 million tons have been found in the southern part of the lowland. The timber reserves in the West Siberian taiga are estimated at 7,500 million cu.m., which exceeds the total reserves of the entire European North.

It is extremely likely that there are concentrations of mineral raw material resources on the eastern slope of the Near-Polar and Polar Urals, which have a structure resembling that of the Central Urals. The so-called gabbro-peridotic formation lies on the eastern slopes of the Urals. In the Central and Northern Urals all the biggest iron ore deposits (Mt. Blagodat and Mt. Vysokaya, the Ivdel mines, etc.) are connected with that formation. Geological research and magnetic surveys have confirmed the assumption that the iron ore belt of the Central and Northern Urals extends far to the north along the eastern slope. It passes from Mt. Vysokaya in the Central Urals to the Rudnaya Gorka deposit in the Polar Urals and continues northward. Granite intrusions are found in the axial part of the Near-Polar and Polar Urals, formed of ancient metamorphic rock. Genetically linked with them are the rock crystal (piezo-quartz) deposits, which are partly exploited, the iron mineralisation and the indications of rare metal and manganese mineralisation. There are also placer deposits of gold, and large reserves of brown coal on the eastern slope.

The economic complex in the north of Western Siberia is growing up mainly on the basis of the above-enumerated resources of the West Siberian Lowland. This territory of an area equal to the whole of Western Europe, with its harsh climate and virtual absence of communications, is developing at a rate and on a scale unprecedented in world practice and in the practice of the development of new areas in the USSR. It is being developed much more quickly than was the Ural-Volga province in its time, although the latter was situated in a densely populated part of the country, an area of traditional settlement with a well-developed communications network. The entire country participates in the task: the efforts of dozens of research and designing organisations have been enlisted, machinery, equipment and building materials are supplied from all parts of the country, many economic organisations (ministries and boards) take part in the region's development in accordance with co-ordinated plans, and tens of thousands of workers and specialists are arriving every year.

The formation of the West Siberian Economic Complex was begun with the development of the area in the central reaches of the Ob—in the Khanty-Mansi National Area and the northern part of Omsk and Tomsk regions. The natural conditions there are more favourable than they are in the tundra, and the territory is more densely populated. The old town of Surgut has become the centre of the oil industry, the base of operations from which the development of the oilfields located further to the north will be launched. Several other important oil centres have emerged, such as Nefteyugansk and Megion. Beryozovo, which has become the centre of the gas industry, is rapidly expanding. New towns and workers' settlements are mushrooming near the oil and gas deposits. The Igrim-Serov-Nizhny Tagil gas pipeline has been built and is supplying Ob gas to the Urals, the Shaim-Tyumen, Ust-Balyk-Omsk oil pipelines have been completed. A railway has been built linking Tyumen with Tobolsk, an old Siberian town that is rapidly becoming the industrial centre of the new region, and is at present being extended to Surgut. The Tyumen-Surgut railway will be the first section of the North Siberian trunk line, later to be extended eastwards to the Pacific coast. Railways have been built to link Ivdel with the Ob station, and Tavda with Sotnik, and the Asino-Bely Yar railway is under construction.

According to the decision of the Central Committee of the CPSU and the Council of Ministers of the USSR, published on January 15, 1970, oil production here is to reach 100-120 million tons in 1975, and 230-260 million tons by 1980—equal to the country's total oil output in 1966. The oil industry is to be supplied with modern equipment, and production processes are to be more fully automated and mechanised. Maximum services and amenities are to be provided for the workers in newly built towns, the construction of housing and communal buildings is to be carried out according to designs taking into account local natural and climatic conditions. An extensive network of roads is to be built, power stations and other infrastructure developments are to be undertaken, while priority is to be given to industrial building. According to estimates, the total volume of the oil and gas production in terms of oil can in the foreseeable future be brought up to 1,000 million tons a year.

Oil and gas production is less labour-intensive than oil-processing and petrochemicals. This being so, it is expedient to locate the enterprises of the latter in the more densely populated districts. It is therefore proposed to develop a large-scale petrochemical industry in the south of the West Siberian Economic Region, based on the raw materials delivered from the north.

New raw material sources and cheap fuel along with the cheap coal of the Itat deposit will make the southern part of Western Siberia a region with a highly developed chemical industry. New big oil, gas and petrochemical complexes are to be built in the south of Tyumen, Tomsk, Novosibirsk and Kemerovo regions.

The prospected oil and gas deposits in the central reaches of the Ob are situated in the taiga zone and their exploitation is therefore bound up with the development of the timber industry.

It is economically expedient to locate timber-processing, especially pulp-and-paper, enterprises near the raw material source. That is because the pulp-and-paper and wood-chemical industries can process the waste and the firewood, comprising over 60 per cent of the total felled timber. In this connection it is planned to build the Verkhne-Kondinskoye and Asino timber industry complexes, which are to include pulp-and-paper mills, saw mills and many other enterprises of the timber-processing industry designed for the complete utilisation of timber. Such complexes, to be set up in Surgut, Kolpashevo, Tobolsk and elsewhere, will process about 30,000,000 cu.m. of timber a year, produce up to 4,000,000 tons of paper and cardboard, up to 5,000,000 cu.m. of saw timber, 1,000,000 cu.m. of plywood, fibre board and various kinds of wood-chemical products. Gas, costing only one-seventh to one-eighth as much as solid fuel, will be used as a power source.

At present over 16,000,000 cu.m. of timber are procured in the Ob North annually. Eventually timber production will be expanded to 45-50,000,000 cu.m. The forests (with a reserve of 2,500 million cu.m.) gravitating towards the newly built Ivdel-Ob railway are being rapidly developed.

In this part of the Ob North the oil and gas industry is being developed in conjunction with the timber industry. The transport network, communications and the infrastructural elements are distributed so as to serve all branches of the economy.

The development of the industrial centres and areas is still in an embryonic state. Many questions of the structure of production are still being debated, and different types of settlements are being considered for the industrial centres to be formed there. The general plan for the development of the entire economic complex will be particularised after the prospecting and design work necessary to find the economically most rational solutions has been completed.

Several big industrial centres, with a large complex of auxiliary and service enterprises, are being built in the middle reaches of the Ob.

The Surgut industrial centre, situated in the centre of the region holding out the greatest prospects for the oil industry and possessing extensive forests, has already become the biggest industrial centre on the middle Ob, with rapidly developing oil and building-material industries and several large mechanised repair workshops. Housing construction has assumed an extensive scale in Surgut.

Within the near future, the annual oil production in the Surgut area is to reach tens of millions of tons and several oil refineries are to be set up there. A big timber complex, designed to process 3-4,000,000 cu. m. of raw materials a year, is under construction. The development of the Surgut district will be promoted by the Tyumen-Surgut railway, to be completed within the next few years. The Ob River is also of great importance in this respect. Surgut will also become the centre of the unique oil and gas deposits situated to the north of it, in the extremely swampy territory of the West Siberian Lowland. A railway is to be built at some later date.

It is not quite clear yet whether the Surgut centre will be a big single industrial centre with a population of 200,000-250,000 or will consist of three to five interlinked industrial nuclei each with a population of 40,000-100,000. A comparison of alternative solutions will enable the question to be resolved in the most rational way.

The Nizhnevartovsk industrial centre is located at a relatively short distance from Surgut and 900 km. from the old university town of Tomsk. Big reserves of oil and gas have been discovered there, and the area is rich in timber. The scale of oil and gas production and the output of the timber industry there will approximately equal that of the Surgut district. The Nizhnevartovsk centre will become the basis for the development of the adjacent Okhteurovskiye and other oil and gas deposits. The present workers' settlement of Nizhnevartovsk will become a town with a population of 120,000-160,000.

The forming Verkhnekondinskoye industrial centre lies on the Ivdel-Ob railway. A big timber complex is to be built there. A large part of the felled timber will be delivered by the Ivdel-Ob railway to the timber-processing enterprises in the Central Urals.

The Igrim-Beryozovo industrial centre is taking shape in the vicinity of the huge natural gas deposits, some of which are already being exploited. The gas is delivered by pipeline to the Urals.

As the development of the natural resources assumes a wider scale, a number of other industrial centres are taking shape on the middle Ob. Yuzhno-Balyk, where the oil industry is already being developed, is one of them.

Tyumen and Tomsk are the bases from which the natural resources of the entire Ob North will be exploited. Building and repair enterprises are being set up there, catering to the needs of the northern territories. Existing research and design institutes are expanding their activities and new ones are being set up. The activity is also intensified of the territorial geological administrations and other organisations connected with the creation of the West Siberian Economic Complex. Tyumen is the main base for the development of the northern part of the West Siberian Lowland.

More and more people are settling in the middle Ob basin, which is being developed most intensively. This makes it very important to set up a local food base. At present agriculture is still being carried on on a very limited scale. At the same time, as already mentioned, climatic conditions favour the growing here not only of vegetables and potatoes, which give good yields, but also of some grain crops—barley, oats and winter rye, suitable for cattle fodder. The hay harvest in the floodlands is 2.0-2.5 tons per hectare, the alluvial soils are very fertile and easily cultivated. The only obstacle is the overflowing of the rivers in spring which sometimes flood these lands for long periods. The cultivation of areas that are not flooded involves heavy expenditure on stubbing the forest-clad land and draining the swamps.

Research has shown that despite considerable difficulties it is economically expedient to develop stock-breeding and to grow potatoes, vegetables and fodder crops in that area. Big state farms, equipped with up-to-date machinery, are being set up for that purpose.

* * *

In the northern part of the West Siberian Lowland the climatic and transport conditions are much worse than those of the middle Ob region. Big gas deposits have been discovered there, including Urengoi, Medvezhye, Tazovskoye, Zapolyarnoye, Vengo-Yakhskoye, Purpeiskoye, Novy Port, etc. High-capacity gas pipelines will be built to take the gas to the European USSR, the Urals, and also possibly to countries neighbouring with the USSR.

The technical plans for the solution of that task have already been drawn up, although the building of pipelines through the tundra involves considerable difficulties and requires the creation of ground communications capable of handling a large goods traffic.

In order to develop the northern gas-bearing district as quickly and cheaply as possible, it is proposed to proceed with building of the Salekhard (Labytnangi)-Igarka railway which was commenced in the early fifties but discontinued in 1953. This was before the big gas deposits were discovered in the region.

The 600-km.-long Salekhard-Urengoi section, along which rails have already been placed, is to be completed first. After that it will be most expedient to continue the road to the Taz River and the Tazovsky gas deposit. Later it will probably be extended to Igarka, where it will link up with the railway that is to connect Norilsk with the Siberian railway network.

As distinct from the industrial centres and districts in the more southward middle Ob area, those in the northern part of the region require a minimum of auxiliary enterprises. The high degree of mechanisation and automation will make it possible to employ fewer workers and technicians. Well-appointed settlements with extensive amenities are to be developed there.

Ukhta and Syktyvkar will be the main bases for the development of the gas deposits in the Yamalo-Nenets National Area. Salekhard, where a big timber complex is being set up, will serve as an intermediate base.

More and more big gas deposits are being discovered every

year. It is expected that oilfields will be found in the Yamal National Area. Their discovery will introduce major changes in the projects for the development of the natural resources in the northern part of the West Siberian economic complex. Among the various development plans, the final choice must be a plan complying with the universally applicable rule that the resources in territories with a severe climate must be tapped with a minimum labour expenditure. The building of the pipelines and the equipment of the gasfields is to be carried out with the help of seasonal teams of workers and engineers, who will live in comfortable hotels, while their families remain at the "supply bases" (Syktyvkar, Tyumen, etc.).

Because of unfavourable natural conditions agriculture will not play an important role there, and will probably be confined to dairy farming.

The further study of the natural resources in the West Siberian Lowland may provide new solutions for the development of the economic complex. However, it is already quite clear that the Ob North will soon become one of the most important industrial regions of the USSR, making a major contribution to the national economy.

The Yenisei North

In the Yenisei North only isolated areas are undergoing development. In the Far North it is still confined primarily to the Norilsk district. Igarka is an important industrial centre and transport hub, while in the southernmost part of the area, at a distance of over 1,500 km. from Igarka, on the Angara river, the timber industry is in full expansion, the 4,300,000-kw. Ust-Ilim hydroelectric power station is under construction, and mining is underway at the big Korshunovo iron ore deposit.

Conditions are favourable for the extensive economic development of the right bank of the Yenisei. It occupies the western part of the Central Siberian Plateau, where Siberian traps are widespread, an indication of the presence of many useful minerals—copper-nickel and iron ore, coal, graphite, optic feldspar and so on. The Central Siberian Plateau is bordered in the west by the Yenisei mountain ridge, extending along the right bank of the Yenisei between

142

the mouths of the Angara and the Podkamennaya Tunguska, and in the north by the Taimyr folded zone, extending from the mouth of the Yenisei to the Khatanga Gulf.

The copper-nickel-cobalt sulphide ores of the Norilsk deposit are of national economic importance. So far only a small part has been prospected, but it is known that identical structures extend to the south and south-east from the ore fields.

Norilsk, in the Taimyr National Area, is a major centre of the copper and nickel industry. It is linked by railway (120 km.) with Dudinka (the centre of the national area), a sea and river port on the Yenisei. The Norilsk combine includes over 20 big coal and polymetallic ore mines and factories processing the ores to obtain nickel, copper, and other valuable metals. Platinoids are the most valuable of the Norilsk ores.

In 1964 development began of the Talnakh copper and nickel deposit, in the immediate vicinity of Norilsk, and the first mines are already operating. The deposit contains ores unique as regards their nickel and copper content. The Dudinka-Norilsk railway has been extended to Talnakh.

Until recently the deposits of Mt. Schmidt and Mt. Nadezhda in the Norilsk coalfields, near the polymetallic ore deposits, provided the fuel for the Norilsk combine. In 1967, the Messoyakha gasfield was discovered on the left bank of the Yenisei, some 270 km. from Norilsk, and in 1969 it began to supply Norilsk with cheap gas, which is to completely replace the expensive local coal.

Prospecting for oil and gas in the Ust-Yeniseisk district and throughout the Taimyr depression holds out great promise. Prospecting for oil is carried on in the eastern part of the Taimyr National Area in the Kozhevnikov and Nordvik bays, and a rich oil deposit has been found in the Yurung-Tumus Peninsula.

Since Norilsk is connected with the other parts of the country only by seasonal water transport, various auxiliary branches of production have been set up there. A big building and repair base has opened up; and the municipal economy has far-flung network of service establishments. In fact, Norilsk is one of the best appointed towns in the Soviet North.

The construction of the hydroelectric power station on

the Khantaika river, in the highest latitude ever attempted so far, will be completed within the next few years. The first units have been put into operation. The foundations of the dam are being laid in permafrost soils. It will supply power to Norilsk and Igarka.

Igarka has three saw mills, part of whose output is exported. Over a hundred sea-going vessels enter its port every year. The raw timber is rafted from the basin of the Angara River to the Igarka. A large part of the export timber arrives on barges from the Maklakovo saw mill near Yeniseisk. Much of the output of the Igarka saw mills goes to Norilsk.

A number of big coalfields have been opened up to the east of the Yenisei. The geological coal reserves in them exceed 25 per cent of the Soviet Union's total coal reserves and make up about two-thirds of the coking coal resources. As yet, however, they are used only on a negligible scale and exclusively for local needs.

The Kureika deposit holds the first place in the USSR as regards the size and quality of graphite reserves. There is also a large graphite deposit on the Nizhnyaya Tunguska. Iceland spar deposits have also been discovered there.

There are goldfields in the Yenisei North. The Yenisei mountain ridge is a very old gold-producing area.

A number of big iron ore (magnetite) deposits have been found in the lower reaches of the Nizhnyaya Tunguska. The ore beds are 20-30 and more metres thick. Several sectors with big magnetite anomalies have been discovered in the neighbourhood. Traces of iron ore have been found on the Kureika River, near Lake Khantaiskoye, on the Makus River and in other places.

The iron ores of the Angara-Ilim basin are of prime importance to the development of the Siberian iron and steel industry. The exploitation has begun here of the Korshunovo (500 million tons) and Rudnogorsk (over 250 million tons) deposits. In the more remote future the iron ore of the Angara-Pit basin, situated to the north of the Angara mouth, is to be utilised. Its forecast reserves are 4,000-5,000 million tons, of which over 2,300 million tons have already been prospected. It is expected that big bauxite deposits will be found in the district between the Angara and the Podkamennaya Tunguska.

The Gorevsk lead-zinc ore deposit, the biggest in the USSR, has been found in the district between the mouth of the Angara and the middle reaches of the Yenisei, where big hydroelectric power stations are to be located.

The Yenisei North possesses considerable timber resources. Much timber is felled in the forests in the Angara area, where reserves run into more than 3,000 million cu.m. These forests, consisting mainly of pine trees, are easily accessible and provide some of the best timber in Siberia. The Angara timber is mainly exported through the port of Igarka, and it is processed at Maklakovo and Yeniseisk. The little explored and as yet untapped forests of the Evenk National Area, the Turukhansk district and the Taimyr National Area, which have vast timber reserves, are situated in the basin of the Podkamennaya Tunguska and to the north of it.

There is an abundance of fish in the lower reaches of the Yenisei, and the forests and tundra of the Ob and Yenisei North abound in fur-bearing animals. The Yenisei North accounts for a large part of the Soviet Union's potential water-power reserves. The potential water-power resources in the lower reaches of the Angara, the middle and lower reaches of the Yenisei, in the Podkamennaya and Nizhnyaya Tunguskas and in the Kureika are calculated at thousands of millions of kwh.

The soil and climatic conditions in the Yenisei North are extremely unfavourable. On the whole, the prospects for the development of agriculture are similar to those of the Ob North, but so far they are less developed here. Crop farming on a very limited scale can be carried on only in the southern part of the territory, mainly on floodlands. At present the sown area is only several hundred hectares, mainly under fodder crops. There are but 2,000 cattle, and even less pigs.

There are two national areas in the Yenisei North. The Evenk National Area (with the settlement of Tura for its centre) occupies an area of 767,600 sq.km. in the basins of the Podkamennaya and Nizhnyaya Tunguska rivers. It has a population of 13,000, of whom urban dwellers account for 4,000, and a density of 16 persons per 1,000 sq.km. The only industrial enterprises there are the Noginsk graphite mines on the Nizhnyaya Tunguska and a few enterprises of local importance. The population engages mainly in hunting and fishing and reindeer-breeding.

The Taimyr (Dolgano-Nenets) National Area (879,300 sq. km.) is situated in the extreme north of the area, within the Arctic Circle. Its main centre is the town of Dudinka. Excluding Norilsk, the population of the area numbers 38,000 people. The native population is made up mainly of Dolgans and Nentsi, but there are also some Yakuts, Entsi, Nganasans and Evenks. The native population engages in reindeer-breeding, hunting and fishing, and fur-farming.

Norilsk, a big industrial and cultural centre, helps to raise the economy of the area and the culture of the native population.

The Turukhansk and Igarka districts, lying between the two national areas, are sparsely populated, mainly by Russians. Outside of the town of Igarka they engage in agriculture, hunting and trapping.

The economy in the Yenisei North is characterised by the presence in the extreme North of two industrial centres (Norilsk and Igarka), the development of forestry and timber-processing in the extreme south and traditional activities (hunting, fishing and reindeer-breeding) carried on extensively over vast tracts of land which are even more sparsely populated than the deserts of Central Asia.

However, industrial development is on the way. It is connected with the utilisation of the vast potential energy of the Angara and the Yenisei, with the tapping of the diverse mineral resources and the extremely rich forests. Cascades of hydroelectric power stations are under construction on these rivers, and their aggregate capacity will ultimately exceed 30,000,000 kw., with over 200,000 million kwh. of electric power being produced annually. Capital investments and cost of the electric power will be at least 60 per cent lower than that of the Volga and Dnieper hydroelectric power stations. Some of these hydroelectric power stations are located in the relatively densely populated southern part of the Krasnoyarsk Territory and Irkutsk region. Big thermal power stations are also being built to operate on cheap Kansk-Achinsk coal, which is mined by the open-cast method. The country's biggest complex of power-intensive enterprises is being set up on the basis of these power stations in the Angara-Yenisei district.

The Angara and Bratsk hydroelectric power stations on the Angara, and the Krasnoyarsk on the Yenisei have already been built, the first open-cast mines are being built in the Kansk-Achinsk coalfields, and big aluminium and chemical plants are being commissioned. The Angara-Yenisei district is gradually becoming the all-Union centre for the concentrated production of power-, heat- and water-intensive kinds of chemical output, aluminium, and a great many other industries.

The 4,300,000-kw. Ust-Ilim hydroelectric power station is under construction in a sparsely populated region of the northern zone. The construction base that served to build the Bratsk hydroelectric power station is used for its erection, and a road has been built from there to Ust-Ilim. A railway line is also under construction. The hydro-electric power station will be commissioned within a few years. Most of electric power produced will be transmitted to the industrial districts of Irkutsk Region and the Kras-noyarsk Territory. A big timber complex is being established near the power station for the production of paper, pulp and other valuable timber products.

One of the high-priority construction projects is the Boguchany hydroelectric power station with its complex of power-intensive enterprises. The forests in the region where the power station is being built have been exploited for many years now. A railway line from Reshety to Bogu-chany is under construction.

A major industrial centre will come into existence on the basis of the Lower Angara and Middle Yenisei hydroelectric power stations, whose total capacity will be not less than 10,000,000 kw. The Gorevsk lead-zinc ore deposit and the Maklakovo timber complex are located in the immediate vicinity of these power stations. Various other industrial enterprises will be set up there.

The Osinovo hydroelectric power station (4,000,000 kw.) is to be built in the near future. A big timber complex is to be set up there and, possibly, some other power-inten-sive industries.

The further the cascade of high-capacity hydroelectric power stations penetrates the unpopulated areas of the north, the stricter must be the choice of enterprises included in the industrial complexes set up around them, and the bigger grows the share of electric power transmitted to the industrial districts of Siberia, to the Urals and the European USSR. Research is therefore being conducted to find opti-mum economic and technical solutions for the transmission of electric power over long distances.

The other hydroelectric power stations of the Yenisei cascade—the Lower Tunguska, Lower Yenisei and others—will apparently be built at a much later date. The entire cascade of hydroelectric power stations on the Angara and Yenisei and the industrial centres around them will probably be completed within the next few decades. This opens up prospects for the eventual creation of a transport network in the Yenisei North.

Other Northern Territories of Eastern Siberia

The Bodaibo goldfields in the basin of the Vitim River, a tributary of the Lena, continue to develop to the east of the Yenisei and the Angara in the north of Irkutsk Region. Even though gold has been mined here for many decades now, there are no indications of it nearing exhaustion. This is a well-equipped industrial area with a number of small hydroelectric power stations and narrow-gauge railways of local importance.

There are copper deposits at Udokan in the north of Chita region, several hundreds kilometres to the north of the Siberian Railway. Development is complicated by the rugged country and harsh climatic conditions. It is intended that the projected North Siberian Railway will pass through the mining area. At a point 900 km. to the east of Udokan it is to cross the railway to be built from the station of Bolshoi Never on the Amur Railway to the north to promote the development of the Chulman coalfield and the Aldan iron ore province. Chulman is to supply coal for the new industrial centre.

The solution of this task, which will be dealt with in greater detail in the following chapter, when we come to examine questions connected with the development of the productive forces in Yakutia, is one of the most important and most urgent problems involved in the development of Siberia's North.

Such are the problems facing the development of the Siberian North today. However, the resources in the territory under review have not yet been sufficiently studied, especially those in the basin of the Yenisei River and to the east of it. The coming years will undoubtedly open up even broader prospects for the development of the Siberian North.

CHAPTER SEVEN
NORTH-EAST USSR

This chapter will deal with the problems involved in the development of the productive forces in the Yakut ASSR, and Magadan and Kamchatka regions which together embrace more than 20 per cent of the territory (4,800,000 sq. km.) of the Soviet Union. The Far East economic region of the USSR, to which we shall refer as the North-East, is emerging as an important economic region. It differs from the other regions of the USSR, including the southern part of the Far East, by a number of distinctive features conditioned by its geographic environment, situation and forms of industrial development.

The natural conditions in the North-East are harsher than in other parts of the North, and it is further removed from the industrialised regions of the country. A large concentration of valuable minerals of national importance has been discovered there, but as yet only isolated areas (oases) are being developed. The area is very sparsely populated (0.6 per cent of the population of the USSR), the majority of the population being concentrated in the industrial and transport centres.

The North-East contains practically 100 per cent of the Soviet Union's known diamond reserves, a large part of its gold, tin, amber mica, natural gas and other valuable minerals. The Sea of Okhotsk and the Bering Sea are important fishing grounds.

In accordance with the general policy of selective industrial development of the natural resources in the North-East, the Yakut ASSR and Magadan Region are specialising in the utilisation of the above-mentioned minerals, whose extraction is economically expedient there, while Kamchatka specialises in the fishing industry, although mining is to be developed there at some future date.

Because of unfavourable natural conditions, agriculture is generally weakly developed. However, in some areas (Central Yakutia, Southern Kamchatka, etc.) it has been carried on for centuries. Local industries and crafts are well developed throughout the North-East and are carried on mainly by the indigenous population.

The high concentration of vast reserves of coal, iron ore, building materials, of some raw materials for food and light industries able to meet the local demand, creates prerequisites for the region's complex economic development and the extension of its production specialisation.

The opening up of the North-East was confined to separate pockets whose development was based on supplies coming from the remote industrialised regions of the country, which reached the North via a complicated transport network, utilising various forms of transport. For a long time there were no economic links between the separate industrial centres of the North-East, lying hundreds and even thousands of kilometres apart. Things are gradually changing in this respect. For example, the emergence in the central districts of Yakutia of a timber industry has made it possible to organise the supply of timber to the economic centres in the Yana and Indigirka basins, to Pevek and even to the Port of Provideniya. The Pevek industrial centre uses coal mined at the Zyryanka deposit on the Kolyma. Thus, links are gradually being established between the various parts of the North-East, and they will grow stronger as its productive forces develop.

A typical feature of the North-East is that the inflow of productive and consumer goods greatly exceeds the outflow of finished products. An analysis of the development of the individual parts of the North-East shows that as the economy grows more diversified and internal economic and transport links grow, it will be possible greatly to reduce the inflow of goods from other districts of the USSR, and gradually reduce this gap.

Let us now examine in turn the three main regions of the North-East: the Yakut ASSR, Magadan Region and Kamchatka Region.

The Yakut ASSR

In tsarist times Yakutia, situated almost 10,000 kilometres from Central Russia and many thousand kilometres from the populated regions of colonial Siberia, was one of the most backward regions of the Russian Empire. There was practically no industry there. The population, concentrated mainly in Central Yakutia, engaged in agriculture, natural economy predominating.

During the years of Soviet power Yakutia advanced industrially and its economy underwent radical restructuring. Yakutia has large diamond, gold, tin, amber mica and natural gas resources. The fur industry is also of national importance. A local industry of republican importance has been set up, a number of good motor roads and winter roads have been built, although a large share of the passenger traffic, and some of the goods traffic, is handled by air transport. Several mining and ore-dressing centres have been set up in the Aldan and Dzhugdzhur districts, along the upper reaches of the Indigirka River, in the Yana river basin and in West Yakutia. The building, ship repair, coal-mining and many other industries are also growing apace.

The remarkable level of industrial development achieved and the increase in the rates at which the republic's natural resources are being exploited can be seen from the following data. Between 1913 and 1965 the aggregate industrial output increased 142 times and doubled in the next five years. The material and technical basis of industry is rapidly growing. Capital investments into the republic's economy have also been growing apace.

Provisional estimates indicate that the mining industry and associate branches account for four-fifths of the industrial fixed assets, labour force and gross output.

Forestry and timber-processing are important. Leather footwear, furniture and other factories have been set up and are working on local raw materials. There are also many small food industry enterprises.

Of Yakutia's total population (664,000 in 1970) the indigenous population, consisting mainly of Yakuts, and also of other northern nationalities (Chukchi, Yukagiri, Evens, Evenks, etc.), accounts for less than 50 per cent. The majority of the indigenous population engages in agriculture and local industries and crafts. Stock-breeding

MINERALS AND INDUSTRIAL CENTRES IN THE YAKUT ASSR

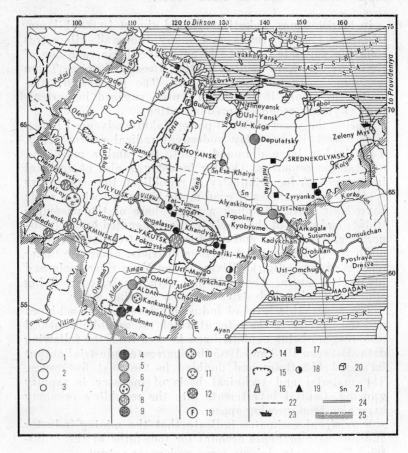

Industrial centres:
1. big 2. medium 3. small
Branches of industry:
4. coal 5. gas 6. ore mining 7. diamond mining 8. timber 9. building materials production 10. mica mining 11. food 12. various
13. fishing
14. Boundaries of coal-bearing areas 15. Boundaries of oil- and gas-bearing areas
Deposits:
16. gas 17. coal 18. gold 19. iron 20. salt 21. tin
22. Main sea routes 23. Ports 24. Motor roads 25. Boundaries of Yakut ASSR

accounts for 75 per cent of the total output of these branches. Meat and dairy farming is carried on on a considerable scale. Horse-breeding for meat production is typical of Yakutia's stock-breeding, and there is a large number of reindeer.

Sown areas, especially under grain crops, have decreased in recent decades because it has been found more economical to bring in grain from southern Siberia. At present mainly fodder crops are sown, and more vegetables and potatoes are being planted, since they are difficult to deliver to these regions as they ripen late in Siberia and the rivers along which they are delivered freeze early.

The fur industry has an important role to play: it accounts (in terms of value) for 11-12 per cent of the total fur procured in the USSR. In addition to the hunting of squirrels, polar foxes, ermine and other fur-bearing animals, fur-farming is widespread in Yakutia. The state fur-farms and the fur-farms run by the collective farms and state farms breed silver foxes, mink and other fur-bearing animals. The output goes to the domestic market and also for export.

Agriculture is concentrated mainly in central Yakutia, while hunting and trapping is carried out throughout the republic, but especially in its northern part.

Considering the vast area of Yakutia, the transport network there is obviously insufficient and this holds up the republic's economic growth. Seasonal forms of transport, operating during the short summer, predominate in the republic's internal and external links—river transport (over 13,000 km.), sea transport (about 2,400 km.), winter roads (10,500 km.) and periodically operating land roads (about 6,000 km.). The total length of surfaced roads and of improved earth roads operating the year round is only 3,700 km. Particularly important among them is the Amur-Yakutia motor road, running from the station of Bolshoi Never on the Amur railway northward through Aldan and Tommot to Yakutsk.

The republic's further economic development is determined by the incidence throughout its territory of extremely valuable minerals—diamonds, tin, gold, etc. The big natural gas deposits are also important to its growth prospects, and it is believed that big oil deposits will be found. The republic has enormous coal reserves, much timber, considerable prospected iron ore reserves in southern Yakutia, and many other minerals. The water-power resources of the Lena River and its tributaries run into tens of millions of kilowatts and power stations can be set up here.

Many of the ore and placer deposits of the above-mentioned valuable minerals contain a higher percentage of the useful component than identical deposits elsewhere in the country, so that despite various cost-raising factors they are mined at a lower cost.

Eventually, after the improvement of the transport system —notably after the building of a railway linking the republic with the country's main railway network—it will become economically expedient to extract gas, high-quality iron ore and coking coal. These minerals will be used not only in the vast area of the USSR to the east of Lake Baikal. They may become a major export item to the countries of the Pacific, and will create a goods traffic running into millions of tons.

As yet only isolated districts are being developed in Yakutia, which accounts for one-seventh of the total area of the USSR. Each of these districts has definite specific economic features and differs considerably from all the others as regards its geographic environment and development prospects. So let us take a look at the development of the most important of these regions.

The South Yakutian (Aldan) mining area embraces a territory of 267,000 sq. km. This is a mountainous country with a harsh climate. In the south and the east it is protected from the Pacific monsoons by the Stanovoi Range but air streams from the polar regions penetrate freely. The Amur-Yakutia motor road, which is the pivot around which the region's life revolves, runs through the territory from the south to the north. A study of the territory near the motor road has shown that it contains vast reserves of diverse minerals. Industrial development was launched in 1923 in connection with the discovery there of rich placer deposits of gold. The placer gold is extracted with drags and mining is fully mechanised.

The prospects for the development of the gold industry in the Aldan region are linked mainly with the discovery there of gold ores. The gold is located close to the surface and some of the deposits can be worked by the open-cast method.

The exploitation of the gold deposits introduces radical changes into the region's development. In the fields where placer gold has been discovered, all structures are temporary because exploitation is confined to a period of a few years. At big gold ore deposits, which are exploited for many decades, well-appointed workers' settlements and production structures are built, creating conditions for the establishment of a permanent population.

The Aldan amber-mica province in southern Yakutia supplies a large share of the amber mica extracted in the USSR. Extraction is carried on at the Emeldzhak and Legrier, Yuzhny and Kuranakh deposits, which are linked by branch roads to the Amur-Yakutia road. Piezo-quartz deposits have also been discovered in the Aldan area. However, their reserves are as yet insufficiently studied and the mining is on a small scale.

The future industrial development of the Aldan mining region is linked with the exploitation of the South Yakutia coalfields (discovered in the early fifties) which have deposits of coking coal of all grades needed for the metal-working industry, and also of the Aldan iron ore province and considerable deposits of non-metallic raw materials for the iron and steel industry. The gold and mica industries are to be considerably expanded.

The problem of using the Aldan iron ores and coking coals has been raised in connection with the necessity of building an iron and steel works to the east of Lake Baikal, to supply metal to the Soviet Far East. It is also possible that coking coals and ferrous metals will be exported to the Pacific countries, especially to Japan.

The southern border of the South Yakutian coalfields runs 380-400 km. to the north of the Bolshoi Never station on the Amur Railway. It extends for about 750 km., occupying an area of 25,000 sq. km. The coalfields as a whole have not yet been fully studied: only the Aldan-Chulman coal-bearing district has been prospected, and ten deposits have been found. The prospected reserves of the Chulmakan and Neryungra deposits are extremely rich.

The coal in both deposits contains little sulphur (0.25-0.6 per cent) and little phosphorites (up to 0.004 per cent), and its ash content is considerable (10-18 per cent). The thickest of the 100 layers discovered at the Neryungra deposit, the Moshchny layer, is 27.5 m. thick. These two

155

deposits can provide all the grades of coal needed for the metallurgical industry.

Tests have proved that the coke obtained from the rich coal in Chulmakan and the thick Moshchny layer in Neryungra is of a very high quality. The mechanical strength of the coke is 330 kg. and it is in no way inferior to Donets coal.

The Chulmakan deposit can be mined by the drift method and the Neryungra deposit by the open-cast method.

Tests have shown that in terms per ton of pig iron the coke from the coal in the Chulman basin costs less than half of the coal from the Bureya basin (the second largest east of Lake Baikal), which was decisive in choosing it as the fuel base for the iron and steel industry.

Several groups of iron ore deposits have been discovered east of Lake Baikal—the Aldan, Priargunsk and Zeya-Selemdzha, and the Maly Khingan. The Aldan province is the biggest of all known iron ore deposits, and contains reserves large enough to supply raw material for a big modern iron and steel works. The province contains mainly magnetite, but some deposits hold also hematite and martite. Best prospected are the Tayozhnoye deposit, with a forecast reserve of 600 million tons, and the Sivanglinskoye and Pionerskoye deposits. The ores contain little phosphorites and, with the exception of those from Tayozhnoye, little sulphur too.

To utilise the coals of the Chulman basin and the Aldan iron ores, it is essential to build a railway that will extend for 600 km. to the north from the station Bolshoi Never on the Amur railway. The railway will be needed for many other purposes. It will transport the coking coal of the Chulman basin intended for export, notably to Japan, where it is in high demand. The Bolshoi Never-Aldan section will become part of the railway trunk line to extend further to the north and north-east, to Yakutsk and the mouth of the Vilyui, where big natural gas deposits have been found, and from Yakutsk eastward to Magadan. It will also become part of the transport system necessary for the exploitation of the big Udokan copper deposit west of Chulman, mentioned in the preceding chapter.

Thus, in the next few years the Aldan mining district will become an important industrial district served by a railway, where there will be iron ore and coal-mining, possibly an iron and steel industry, and the gold (mainly on the basis of gold ore) and the mica industry will be further developed. Some auxiliary branches of production will arise, although their prospects are very limited. Thus, it will probably be more expedient to bring in consumer goods, including also a large part of the agricultural supplies, from Amur Region and other parts of the country.

Western Yakutia embraces the eastern part of the Central Siberian Plateau. While geological surveying is still far from complete, it has been established that it contains the biggest diamond-bearing province in the world, as well as coal, salt and gas, and many other valuable minerals are likely to be discovered.

The most populated areas of Western Yakutia are in the south and near the Lena where there is some forestry and relatively well-developed agriculture, the latter carried on mainly by the indigenous population.

In Western Yakutia one can distinguish two separate areas, with poor communications between them: the Vilyui basin and the lands of the Lena drainage to the south, and the basins of the Olenyok and Anabar rivers, the latter being among those having the harshest climatic conditions and lowest population density in Yakutia.

Western Yakutia's industrial development is linked with the exploitation of the rich resources in the Vilyui basin, which has an area of 480,000 sq.km. and is very sparsely populated. The western part of the basin (the upper and middle reaches of the Vilyui) lies in the south-eastern part of the Central Siberian Plateau, where the highest elevation at the watershed between the Vilyui and the Olenyok rivers reaches 850-900 m. The eastern part of the basin (the lower reaches of the Vilyui and its tributaries) lies at a low altitude (the Lena-Vilyui lowland), and contains numerous swampy areas and lakes.

In the Vilyui district agriculture is very poorly developed, and a large part of the produce (meat and vegetables) is brought in from central Yakutia. As a result, the links between these districts are expanding.

The basins of the Olenyok and Anabar rivers are divided from the Vilyui district by a watershed. The sparse native population carries on various northern crafts and trades. Of the district's natural resources only the bogheads on the Olenyok river (Taimylyr and other deposits) have been prospected so far. The geological survey of the district indicates that it is likely that oil-bearing strata will be found in the area between the lower reaches of the Anabar and Lena rivers. Placer deposits of valuable minerals have been discovered in the Anabar and Olenyok basins. On the whole, however, the area has as yet been insufficiently studied.

The Olenyok River can be reached via the Lena and the Olenyok channel and sea-going vessels can approach the mouth of the Anabar. Both rivers are too shallow for navigation by any but small craft.

The central region of the Yakut ASSR embraces a large part of the right bank of the Lena, the territory between the Lena and the Aldan and the south-west of the republic. This is the most populated district in Yakutia and agriculture is best developed there. The town of Yakutsk has long since become an important transport junction. In the Soviet period there has been extensive (considering local conditions) industrial development there. In view of the rich natural resources the prospects for industrial advance look most promising.

The Yakut ASSR has vast timber resources, mainly in the central and south-western parts of the republic, eighty-six per cent of the forests being made up of Dahurian larch. The timber is used mainly for local needs, because of remoteness from large-scale consumers, although a small amount of Dahurian larch is exported along the Northern Sea Route to Japan. The export of larch should be given greater attention since it is in high demand on the world market. At present the volume of timber procured and processed is still small.

Limestone, quartzes, sands, clays, gypsum and other raw materials for the building industry have been found along the middle reaches of the Lena. A big construction base is being set up near the town of Pokrovsk, where brick and reinforced concrete elements are being produced, and a cement factory and other enterprises for the production of building materials have been built.

Building materials and finished structural units can be brought from the central part of Yakutia to the Yana, Indigirka and Kolyma basins, and to the Pevek industrial district by the waterways in the Lena basin and some sections of the Northern Sea Route. After the completion of the motor road leading from Khandyga to Kadykchan and the roads to the Ust-Nera and Burgochan districts (which will be discussed later), the above-mentioned construction base will supply the north-east of the republic and to some extent also the western part of Magadan Region.

The exploitation of the natural gas deposits in the mouth of the Vilyui and to the south-west of it, the forecast reserves of which exceed 13 trillion cu.m., will exert a major impact on the industrialisation of the republic and living conditions there. A 45-km. gas pipeline has been completed from the mouth of the Vilyui to Yakutsk, and already supplies power stations and the town of Yakutsk, as well as the populated centres along its path. Computations show that the saving on fuel costs and reduction of the number of workers employed in the coal industry alone will recoup the outlay on the building of the pipeline in 5-6 years. The high condensation of the gas makes it expedient to build a plant for the production of kerosene, gasoline and diesel oil.

Yakutian gas is important not only to the republic. Firstly, since the utilisation of large-diameter pipes makes it possible to convey gas over vast distances at comparatively low cost, this opens up the prospect of supplying gas to the southern districts of the Far East. Secondly, there is the possibility of exporting liquefied gas to the countries of the Pacific Basin, notably to Japan. A plant for liquefying gas could be built in the south of the Far East, near a seaport.

Geological surveys give reason to believe that a large oil-bearing province will be found in the Verkhoyansk flexure. When that province is found, the question may arise of supplying Yakutian oil to the southern districts of the Far East. Calculations have shown that even if the Yakutian oil is much more expensive than the West Siberian, the total cost, including transportation, may turn out to be lower.

The building of the Bolshoi Never-Aldan railway, and its subsequent extension to Yakutsk, is of great importance to the industrialisation of the central part of Yakutia. The railway will give a new impetus to industrial development in the republic.

Best prospected among the rock salt deposits and salt sources in the south-west of the republic is the Solyanka deposit near the town of Olyokminsk. Here nine layers have been found, with an average thickness of 3.19-13.2 m. each. The salt is of a high quality, and can be used for the fishing industry, for foods and also for technological purposes. Permafrost extends to a depth of 100 m., which facilitates underground mining. However, the problem of using the Olyokminsk salt is still under discussion, since the exploitation of the deposits will involve heavy transport construction. Geological prospecting for oil deposits continues. Their discovery will improve the district's prospects for economic development, especially since it has a relatively favourable climate.

The north-eastern industrial district of the Yakut ASSR embraces the basins of the Yana, Indigirka and Kolyma (in its middle and lower reaches).

The Yana river basin is the main tin-bearing district in the USSR. Three groups of tin deposits are found there:

(a) The northern group, including the placer and primary tin deposits in the region of the Polousny ridge between the Yana and Indigirka rivers. The placer deposits in the basin of the Deputatskaya river and its tributaries have been exploited since 1951. Dressing costs are the lowest in the north. All arduous processes at the mines are mechanised. In recent years the exploitation of the big primary deposit has been intensified. A dressing combine is under construction. The ore contains various valuable components—lead, zinc and others.

Some way off to the north-east from these deposits are a number of as yet little-prospected non-ferrous metal deposits. The Kular goldfield is already being exploited.

The Deputatskaya deposit is most accessible from the side of the Yana River (the Kuiga landing stage). Cargoes are taken through the mouth of the Yana by water as far as Kuiga, where they are reloaded onto lorries travelling along the winter road;

(b) The central group, which includes the primary deposit at Ese-Khaiya, being exploited since 1941. An ore-dressing plant has been built in Batagai, which is linked with the mine by a motor road. Supplies are delivered through the mouth of the Yana to Batagai. Some are transported by the winter road from the Khandyga on the Aldan River;

(c) The southern group, including the Ilin-Tas, Burgochan, Alys-Khaiya and other deposits. These deposits contain complex ores.

Placing of concrete on the Kolyma motor road

Through the ice of the Sea of Okhotsk

Arctic styles

A lesson in the vernacular at the boarding school in the village of Lorino in the Chukotka National Area

The village of Bilibino in the Chukotka National Area. The first atomic power plant is being built near that village

Old and new monuments to the Russian explorer Semyon Dezhnev at Mys Dezhneva, North-East Asia's most remote point

Lenin Square in the town of Magadan

Exploitation of the tin deposits in the Yana basin is linked with the general development trends of the Soviet tin industry and a comparative technico-economic evaluation of the prospected tin deposits in the Soviet North-East, Eastern Siberia and the Soviet Far East.

Rich placer deposits of gold have been found along the upper reaches of the Indigirka, and mining was begun in 1944. The gold-mining centre is Ust-Nera on the Kolyma motor road, which has branch roads leading to the mines. The Ust-Nera district maintains close economic links with Magadan Region, which are to continue to develop.

At present all goods coming to the area from the European USSR and Siberia are first transported by railway to the Far Eastern ports, then by sea to the port of Nagayevo, and, finally, by the Kolyma motor road to Ust-Nera. The total distance travelled by Siberian freight (as from Novosibirsk) is 10,000 km. If the capacity of the Khandyga-Kadykchan motor road is increased to that of the Kolyma motor road, and a 140-km. motor road is built from the Kobyume settlement, situated on that road, to the Marshalsky settlement, cargoes can be delivered to the Verkhnyaya Indigirka by a shorter and cheaper way. European and Siberian freight loads could be sent by railway to Osetrovo, by the Lena and Aldan to Khandyga and thence by motor road to Ust-Nera. In that case the total run would be 5,000 km., half the distance of the present route, and the transport costs would be reduced by as much as 50 rubles per ton.

These motor roads will be built within the next few years. They will be used to deliver goods not only to the Verkhnyaya Indigirka district but also to a large part of the gold industry enterprises in the west of Magadan Region.

In its middle and lower reaches, that is below Mama, where navigation is possible, the basin of the Indigirka River is extremely thinly populated. The natural resources of the district have not been sufficiently studied, and industry is undeveloped. The big coal deposits found there will not be exploited in the near future.

In the central and lower parts of the Kolyma basin, which form part of the Yakut ASSR, coal is mined at Zyryanka. It is used, in particular, as fuel in the port and settlement of Pevek. This part of north-eastern Yakutia has close economic links with Magadan Region and will be described in greater detail in the following section.

All the above shows that the Yakut ASSR will become a region with a developed industry and transport network. A number of industrial districts will be set up there. Yakutia's population will grow as its industry and transport develop.

Magadan Region

Magadan Region was formed in 1953. The region has a territory of 1,199,100 sq.km., of which the Chukotka National Area, forming part of it, accounts for 737,700 sq.km. The region extends about 1,000 km. from north to south and for 1,500 km. at its widest part from west to east. It is the area of the USSR most remote from the Central districts, and in the north-east has a sea border with Alaska. The distance from Moscow to Magadan, the region's administrative centre, is 10,500 km. Magadan Region is one of the biggest yet most sparsely populated regions in the country, with 352,000 inhabitants (1970). The density is 0.3 per 1 sq.km., and 75 per cent of the population is concentrated in the town of Magadan (92,000) and in numerous workers' settlements.

Despite its small population Magadan Region is one of the Soviet Union's important industrial areas. The economic structure is determined first and foremost by its big share in the country's gold- and tin-mining. The region is called the country's "gold factory". Although less important, the fishing industry is also developed. The native population— the Chukchi, Eskimos, Koryaks, Evens and other northern nationalities are engaged in reindeer-breeding, hunting, trapping and fishing.

The economico-geographic situation of the region is determined by its extensive coastline and the absence of land communications with the other parts of the country. Since it is practically accessible only by sea, Magadan Region, like the other north-eastern districts, can be regarded as an island. The seas washing the shores of Magadan Region are ice-bound much of the year and navigation without the help of ice-breakers is possible only during 5-7 months, and in the Arctic seas for only 3-4 months a year. The chief port—Nagayevo—is ice-bound practically all the year round and can be reached only with the help of ice-breakers. The enormous distances and the long time it takes to deliver goods by sea greatly hamper the delivery of supplies.

The region has mountain ranges, extensive plateaus and a few depressions. The climate is extremely harsh—it is dry and cold in winter when the minimum temperature reaches minus 65°C, cool and wet in summer. Permafrost spreads practically through the entire territory, and it is only in its southern parts that areas with thawed soil are found.

The mountainous terrain, gley and gleyly-swamp soils, the cold climate and, in many places, extremely low precipitation, hamper the development of agriculture. Only in the south of the region (Olsk district), in some sections along the Kolyma motor road, and in the basin of the Anadyr River (mainly around the village of Markovo) can some vegetables and potatoes be grown on open ground, and dairy cattle bred. The natural conditions in the region, especially in its northern part, favour reindeer-breeding. Extensive tundra overgrown with reindeer-lichen provides fodder for the herds.

Geological prospecting has revealed that two large metallogenic belts extend over a large part of the North-East of the USSR. The so-called main Verkhoyansk-Kolyma gold-bearing belt extends across Magadan Region from the south-east to the north-west passing through the upper reaches of the Kolyma. Placer gold deposits are concentrated also in the north of Chukotka. A stanniferous belt extends from the lower reaches of the Yana and Indigirka to the east, crossing the northern part of the Chukotka National Area. A number of tin and tin-tungsten deposits are found there.

South of the Verkhoyansk-Kolyma gold-bearing belt, a wide molybdenum belt extends for thousands of kilometres from west to east and north-east. Industrial surveying is yet to be made.

Mercury deposits have been found in the north of Chukotka and in the area of the Koryak range.

The above metallogenic areas contain not only numerous gold, tin and tungsten deposits, but also many other valuable minerals, for example, zinc and lead. The tin ore in many deposits contains also many other valuable components.

11*

Numerous coalfields have been found in Magadan Region, many of them are already being worked. These are the Arkagala, Beringovsky and Anadyr deposits where over 2,000,000 tons of coal are mined a year. Various raw materials for the production of building materials have also been found. As regards its natural resources, Magadan Region is one of the richest in the USSR.

Before the Revolution there was no industry whatever on the territory forming Magadan Region: the indigenous population engaged in reindeer-breeding and hunting in the tundra and taiga, and in sea-mammal hunting and fishing in the coastal areas. The population numbered only 20,000, consisting mainly of the small northern nationalities and a few Russians. The shore dwellers (mainly Chukchi) led a sedentary life, while the majority of the population, engaging in reindeer-breeding and hunting, were nomads. The natural resources of the region had hardly been studied at all.

Soviet power was established in the North-East in 1923 after the White bands and interventionists had been driven out. In 1926 a geological expedition headed by S. V. Obruchev was working there. In 1928 the Geological Committee organised the first Kolyma expedition under Y. A. Bilibin, which discovered gold in the extreme North-East. In 1928-1929 gold deposits were discovered in the upper reaches of the Kolyma. Bilibin's prediction that a large gold-bearing province would be found along the upper reaches of the Kolyma came true. The first goldmines were organised there in 1930.

The industrial development of the territory's natural resources began in the east and gradually spread to the north and north-west (see map on opposite page). The port of Nagayevo was built, and it became the trans-shipment centre for goods necessary to develop the territory and to supply the quickly growing population. The town of Magadan which mushroomed into being next to the port became the supply base, from which the development of the taiga was launched. First to be tapped were the big placer deposits with an exceedingly high gold content. The motor road from Nagayevo to the north and north-west was built in the direction of the newly discovered deposits. A network of roads was built to embrace the main gold-bearing belt in the upper reaches of the Kolyma and Indigirka. Then a group of tin deposits was found in the area of Omsukchan, which was

INDUSTRIAL DEVELOPMENT AND TRANSPORTATION
IN MAGADAN REGION

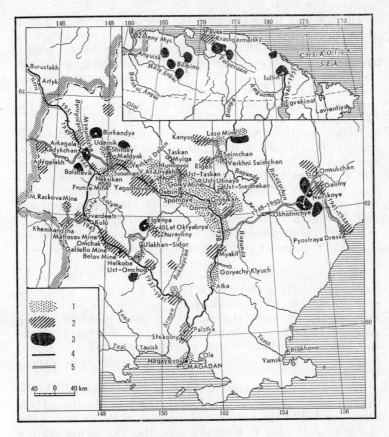

Development periods: 1—1932-1940; 2—1941-1950; 3—1951-1968;
4—motor roads; 5—temporary motor roads

not connected with the Kolyma motor road. A road was
therefore built from the new landing stage at Pyostraya
Dresva to Omsukchan. However, unfavourable navigational conditions hampered the utilisation of that road and
a branch was built to link Gerba on the Kolyma motor
road with Omsukchan to the east of it. The total length
of the motor road in that part of the region exceeds

4,500 km. Magadan Region has thousands of lorries, and repair stations, warehouses and petrol stations have been built on the roads.

The Kolyma Road traverses the southern part of Magadan Region, leading from the port of Nagayevo northward to Ust-Nera (Yakut ASSR). A more than 500-km. branch makes a loop through the extensive gold-bearing district and comes back to the main road. Several workers' settlements, including Susuman and Orotukan, lying along this road loop at long intervals are the supply bases for the development of that remote territory.

Motor repair stations have been built in Magadan and Sporny, plants for the repair of mining equipment in Magadan and Orotukan, central repair workshops in Susuman and Pevek, and also a number of repair workshops at the vehicle depots. These enterprises have the equipment necessary to carry out major overhauls of vehicles of different models and all the necessary spare parts. A small plant in Orotukan produces steels of different grades needed for the repair of motor vehicles and equipment, and for construction.

The Arkagala power station, a big one for the North, has been operating there since 1954 on local coal. A network of high-tension transmission lines supplies the main gold-mining district with electric power. The building of the power station had made it possible to close many of the small power stations, which operated on wood and liquid fuel brought from afar, and were therefore far more expensive to run.

Tin deposits discovered in 1936 in the district of Chaunskaya Guba have been mined since the late thirties. Their discovery led to the building of the port of Pevek and of the motor road linking it with the deposits. The power station in Pevek supplies the entire district. In 1959 a mine and a dressing plant were opened at the Iultin tin-tungsten deposit, and a well-appointed workers' settlement has sprung up in the deserted mountainous district. It was necessary to build the port of Egvekinot in Krest Bay, a motor road from the port to the deposit and a power station operating on coal from the Beringovsky deposit.

In the thirties a seaport was built in Provideniya Bay. It is the most important Arctic port in the east, where sea vessels take on supplies of coal and fresh water.

The extremely high gold content in the sands at the placer deposits along the upper reaches of the Kolyma and Indigirka and its mining on a large scale lower the cost of the metal obtained there, and this makes it economically expedient to exploit the northern deposits despite the harsh climate. This also justifies the big capital outlay on the industrial development of the gold and tin deposits, the building of roads, of the town of Magadan and the workers' settlements as well as the state farms and auxiliary agricultural enterprises around it.

A look at the present state of the economy and the composition of the population in Magadan Region shows that it is still a region of pioneer development with considerable differences in the economic level of different areas. Typical of the region as a whole is high urban concentration, mainly accounted for by people who have arrived there on contract from other parts of the country (the mechanical increment accounts for 90 per cent of the total population increase in the region). There is a heavy preponderance of males, and the proportion of single people and people with small families is very high. Over 75 per cent of the working population is below 40 and only 8 per cent is 50 and over. The share of young people is very high. People reaching a pensionable age generally leave for parts with a more favourable climate. All these indicators are even more clearly pronounced in the Chukotka National Area, where intensive industrial development is fairly recent. One should also note the large proportion of specialists with a secondary and a higher education among the population, which is much bigger than in the Far East Economic Region as a whole. A large share of the population is engaged in geological prospecting.

Most of the economic branches there (fuel and power, engineering, metal-working, etc.) are linked with the development of the non-ferrous metals industry, the region's specialisation, which together with ancillary branches employs four-fifths of the industrial labour force.

The fishing industry comes a poor second with about 7 per cent of labour force employed in it. The share of the region in the total Soviet catch is small, about one-tenth that of neighbouring Kamchatka.

Because of the harsh natural conditions crop farming is very weakly developed. Most of the sown areas are in the

167

southern part of the region. The number of cattle (dairy and meat) is gradually increasing. Poultry-farming is also gradually coming into its own. Magadan Region holds the first place in the Soviet Union for reindeer-breeding, one-third of the total. Reindeer-breeding is particularly well-developed in the Chukotka National Area. Besides reindeer-breeding, fur-farming, fishing and the hunting of sea mammals are the main occupations of the native population—the Chukchi, Evens, Evenks and others. The fur-farms are concentrated mainly in the Chukotka National Area, where wastes from reindeer-breeding and sea-animal hunting provide the necessary feed.

The region is divided into two economic districts: the Kolyma-Magadan (or Central), in the southern part, and the Chukotka, embracing the territory of the Chukotka National Area.

The Kolyma-Magadan Economic Region is industrialised. It was here that the initial development of Magadan Region was begun 40 years ago. Its specialisation in the all-Union division of labour is determined by the mining of gold and, on a smaller scale, of tin, and the utilisation of the fish resources of the Sea of Okhotsk. The district has an important role to play in the industrial development of the more remote northern territories of Magadan Region.

The district is relatively densely populated, containing four-fifths of Magadan Region's total population. The native population lives mainly in the Olsk and North-Even districts.

Transportation pivots upon the Kolyma motor road with its branch roads and the port of Nagayevo. The district includes the territory gravitating towards the above transport network and contiguous areas where industry and transport are likely to be developed in the not-so-distant future.

The district can be divided into three sub-districts, which are interlinked, but differ as regards their economic development. They are the Verkhnyaya Kolyma gold-mining area, the Omsukchan tin-mining area and the Magadan transport-industrial centre.

The first-named embraces the main gold-bearing belt. It includes all the goldfields, a number of centres with repair enterprises, motor depots, warehouses (Susuman, Tinka, Yagodnoye, Orotukan, Ust-Omchug, etc.). They are connected with one another and with the Magadan centre by a network of roads.

The Orbita TV station in Magadan. It relays Moscow TV programmes beamed via the Molniya artificial communications satellite to the homes of Magadan televiewers

The transmission lines taking power from the Arkagalinsk power plant to all the goldfields in Magadan Region traverse two thousand kilometres in mountainous country

Fishing port in the town of Petropavlovsk-Kamchatsky

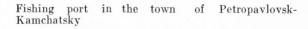

Magadan Region. Workers' settlement of the Duncha poultrybreeding state farm

The 4,850-metre Khyuchevskaya Sopka volcano, the tallest in Kamchatka

The famed geyser valley in the south of Kamchatka

Construction of the first geothermal electric power plant on the Pauzhetsky springs in Kamchatka, which is already operative

A concert by the Koryak amateur dance company "Mengo"

"Mengo" en route

Kamchatka Region. A tourist camp in the geyser valley

Magadan Region is probably the only major gold-bearing region in the world where gold is still extracted mainly at placer deposits (up to 97 per cent). Their exploitation is extremely profitable because relatively small capital investments are required. However, the gradual exhaustion of the highly productive placers and the need to increase gold production raises a number of new problems.

Thus, ways are being sought to make the working of the placer deposits more economical. Experience has shown that it is impractical to build permanent structures at deposits that are exhausted in 5-15 years. The emphasis is thus on buildings which take only a few days to assemble or dismantle, so that when a deposit is exhausted they can be rapidly dismantled and set up at a new deposit. The use of prefabricated structural units made of modern light materials can reduce capital outlay on building at mines to between one-fifth and one-sixth to what it was. Temporary structures are also most convenient for geological prospecting.

A factory for building elements and structural units of light-weight materials (aluminium, plastics, plywood, etc.) for the construction of temporary production buildings and housing is now nearing completion in Magadan. They will be delivered by plane and helicopter to remote districts difficult of access and to small deposits lying far from motor roads.

The factory will supply not only the gold and tin industry in the Kolyma-Magadan district, but will become an important supply base for the whole of Magadan Region.

In Magadan Region, and especially in the area under review, there are buried placers at a depth of 50-200 metres. They are worked by the drift method. Although drift mining involves greater expenditure it has also certain advantages. One is that work continues throughout the winter, while the washing of sands on the surface is impossible in winter because of the frost.

Utilisation of the remaining big reserves of gold in the placer deposits in the Verkhnyaya Kolyma area will only be economically expedient if ore-processing is carried out on a large scale.

On the whole, there are sufficient reserves to continue mining for a long time to come. If cheap electric power were available, more gold could be mined and more effective methods could be applied. In this connection it has been decided to build a number of big power stations in Magadan Region. Hydroelectric power stations will be built within the next five years in the middle reaches of the Kolyma by decision of the 24th Congress of the CPSU, and the projects for the building of atomic power stations of medium and low capacity also deserve attention.

The share of Verkhnyaya Kolyma in the gold output of Magadan Region will gradually drop as new gold-bearing areas are developed in the north of the region. However, output will increase in absolute terms because of the utilisation of numerous small, but rich placer deposits of gold, buried placers and ore deposits. The tapping of ore deposits will lead to the setting-up of new permanent workers' settlements with permanent well-appointed houses, communal and productive structures.

The Omsukchan sub-district embraces the territory of the Omsukchan administrative district, including a small tin-mining centre, with several small tin mines and a group of ancillary enterprises (coal mines, a power station, etc.). The majority of the population is concentrated in the settlement of Omsukchan. The area gravitates around two motor roads linking it with the other parts of the country: the Pyostraya Dresva-Omsukchan and the Gerba (on the Kolyma road)-Omsukchan roads.

As present knowledge of the area's resources stands, development will be limited to the exploitation of a prospected group of small but rich tin deposits.

The Magadan sub-district comprises the territory around the Magadan transport-industrial centre, consisting of the town of Magadan and the port of Nagayevo, and also the Olsk administrative district and the North-Even National District.

The port and the town form the most important transport and distribution centre in Magadan Region. At present all freight for the Kolyma-Magadan economic district pass through the port of Nagayevo.

The town of Magadan has repair plants, which may be considered large for the North, a cement factory, several small local industrial enterprises. Magadan is the administrative, economic and cultural centre of the region. It lies about 500 km. from the main gold-mining districts.

The Chukotka Economic Region is growing in importance.

in connection with the mining of gold, tin, tungsten and mercury. It is expected that other valuable minerals will be found in the North Chukotka metallogenic belt.

The rich placer deposits of gold in the basins of the Bolshoi and Maly Anyui rivers have been exploited since 1958. The urban-type settlement of Bilibino, named in honour of the discoverer of gold in the extreme North-East, is the centre of the goldfields. The port of Zeleny Mys, built in the lower reaches of the Kolyma, can accommodate small sea-going vessels. An atomic power station is nearing completion at Bilibino, and is to produce enough electricity to supply the entire gold-bearing district.

As we noted above, the completion of the seaport of Pevek in the late 1930s coincided with the beginning of the exploitation of the gold and tin deposits in the district orientated towards the port. This led to the building of the road to the Valkumei tin mine and the tin deposits to the south of Pevek (Krasnoarmeisky, Pyrkakai and others). New gold and mercury deposits have been developed in recent years.

A motor road is to be built from Zeleny Mys to the east, which will operate all year round and will replace the present winter road. Since the gold deposits are to the north-east of Bilibino, the two motor roads (from Zeleny Mys to the east, and from Pevek to the south) will be linked up in the near future, bringing about the formation of a Chaun-Chukotka non-ferrous metal-smelting district. The Bilibino atomic power station will be linked by a transmission line with the Pevek power station and create the north-western power grid.

The Iultin tin-tungsten industry centre, linked by a motor road with the port of Egvekinot, has been built in the extreme east of Magadan Region. There are geological indications that many valuable mineral deposits will be discovered there.

A new mining centre has emerged in the area of Mys Schmidta. Some deposits are already being worked there, and new ones are being discovered. The motor road from Iultin will be extended to the new centre.

Discoveries of new deposits in the metallogenic belt in the northern part of the Chukotka National Area will make it necessary to build a network of roads, most important of which will be the trunk road from Zeleny Mys via Bilibino, Krasnoarmeisky and Iultin to the port of Egvekinot in the east. In the nearest future a new industrial area, resembling in many respects Verkhnyaya Kolyma, will take shape here.

The Port of Provideniya. This convenient port in Providetniya Bay is the region's main eastern Arctic sea outlet. Ships sailing the Northern Sea Route take on coal and fresh water here. It also serves as the homeport for ships handling local transfers. Now that sea vessels operate on liquid fuel, the importance of the port as a coaling base has diminished; however it is to become an important trans-shipment base in the Northern Sea Route system. The warehousing of cargoes there will enable transport vessels to make two or three trips through the Arctic seas during the short navigational period.

Anadyr is the centre of the Chukotka National Area. Fishing is developed on a moderate scale, and there are a few coal mines in the neighbourhood. Gold deposits have been discovered to the south of Anadyr.

Geological surveying and prospecting for oil has been carried on in the Anadyr basin for a number of years now. According to the forecasts of prominent geologists, notably of Academician A. A. Trofimuk, it is expected that an oil-bearing province with considerable reserves will be discovered there. This would open up broad prospects for the industrial development of the Chukotka National Area.

This warrants the conclusion that the economic development in Magadan Region displays the following tendencies:

1. For many years to come the region will remain one of the country's main gold-mining districts.

2. The prospects of the tin-mining are linked mainly with the exploitation of big deposits.

3. The production of a sufficient amount of cheap electric power will be decisive in the further development of the region's main economic branches.

4. Geological prospecting is far from complete and future discoveries may provide an impetus for new economic development trends.

5. The population will continue to grow since development will spread to ever new parts of the vast and thinly populated territory.

6. The North-Eastern railway, which is to be built within the next 15-20 years, will revolutionise the region's economy.

Magadan Region is a new land with vast prospects of development.

Kamchatka Region

General

Kamchatka Region, embracing the Kamchatka Peninsula, is one of the most remote parts of the USSR. It is extremely picturesque, and very special as regards its natural and economic conditions. Kamchatka is famous for its beautiful Avachinskaya Bay, which does not freeze in winter, is protected against winds and is large enough to accommodate a large part of the world's fleet. It is also famous for its salmon and other valuable breeds of fish, for the crabs in the mouths of its rivers and inshore waters, for its many volcanos, of which some 15 are active, and for its hot springs of volcanic origin. The natural resources of the region have as yet been insufficiently studied, and further research is necessary to define its economic development prospects more precisely.

The region's specialisation in the inter-regional division of labour is one-sided as yet, and is confined mainly to the fishing industry. Gold-mining has begun there only recently. Besides Kamchatka has become a tourist mecca, popular with nature lovers from all over the country.

Kamchatka Region occupies an area of 472,000 sq. km., of which 301,500 sq. km. form the Koryak National Area. The population numbers correspondingly 287,000 and 31,000, the average population density—0.6 and 0.1 per 1 sq.km. Most of the population lives in the southern part of the peninsula, which has a milder climate. Practically all the fishing industry, repair workshops and agriculture are concentrated there. The Koryak National Area, in the north of the region, has long been inhabited by the Koryaks, Itelmens and Evens, who engage in fishing, hunting and reindeer-breeding. The valley of the Kamchatka River, over 500 km. long and from 4 to 100 km. wide, is protected by the mountain ranges and has a very favourable micro-climate. As distinct from the rest of Kamchatka, which is mainly overgrown with dwarf lichen, there are beautiful pine forests there, and the land is sown not only to potatoes and vegetables, which yield excellent harvests, but also to grain crops, including wheat suited to warm climates. About 400,000 cu.m. of timber is felled in the valley every year and is floated down the river to the sawmill at Ust-Kamchatsk.

The seas washing the shores of Kamchatka abound in fish. All known salmon species, herring, flatfish, cod, and other fishes are caught there. The north-western and north-eastern parts of the Pacific Ocean have especially rich fishing grounds.

The mineral resources of Kamchatka have as yet been inadequately studied. There is some prospecting for oil and gas, and geological data obtained so far warrants the hope that big gold reserves will be discovered. Many sulphur deposits have been found. Mercury deposits have been discovered in the northern part of the Koryak National Area. There are many deposits of coal, both bituminous and lignite, and peat reserves, especially in the south-western part of the peninsula, which is partly used as fuel. Kamchatka is rich in hot mineral springs.

Fishing

Kamchatka is one of the country's most important centres of the fishing industry. It accounts for 9-10 per cent of the total catch in the USSR, and almost 100 per cent of the canned crab. In the Soviet Far East, it accounts for 30 per cent of the total catch and 25 per cent of the canned fish. Labour productivity is higher than in other parts of the USSR, and the produce is of extremely high quality. At the same time the cost of the fish products made in Kamchatka is higher than in other parts of the Far East, because wages are higher (the special Northern rating).

In recent years the fish-processing enterprises have been reorganised into big combines with powerful high-capacity refrigeration installations, canning and salting plants, and also factories for the utilisation of by-products (oil, fish flour, proteins, vitamins). Yet, the processing cost at the combines is several times higher than on big trawlers and floating fish-factories. Therefore, most of the catch is reloaded from small and medium vessels to big floating fish-factories.

Minerals

Geological surveying carried out to date in Kamchatka and its geological structure hold out the prospect that some of its minerals will soon be exploited.

Oil was first discovered in Kamchatka in 1921. Recent geological research has established that oil is found not only in paleogenic Tertiary formations, but also in neogenic rocks, of a kind similar to those of the oil deposits being exploited on Sakhalin. This seems to promise that more oil will be discovered, which may be of great practical importance to the region.

The oil in the Bogachevka deposit belongs to the light type, containing a high percentage of gasoline-ligroine fractions. According to the estimates of the All-Union Geological Surveying Research Institute, the forecast oil reserves on Kamchatka run into approximately 300 million tons.

The recently found placer deposits of gold are also of commercial importance. Some of them are being worked. Geological forecasts suggest that a gold-bearing province will probably be discovered there and gold-mining will be greatly increased.

Mercury is an extremely valuable but scarce metal. This attaches particular importance to the discovery of a new mercury-bearing province in Kamchatka Region. The exploitation of the great forecast reserves of mercury in the Koryak upland would make Kamchatka a major mercury-mining district in future. Information on the general nature of the mercury mineralisation, on the metal content of the ore and also on the bedding of some of the mercury bodies warrant the conclusion that the mining of mercury is economically expedient.

The question of utilising the numerous sulphur deposits, some of which are estimated to be large, is also worth studying.

Copper has been discovered in fifty places throughout the region, and copper deposits may also become commercially important in future. Numerous outcrops of molybdenum have also been found in the copper zone.

MINERALS AND INDUSTRIAL CENTRES
IN KAMCHATKA REGION

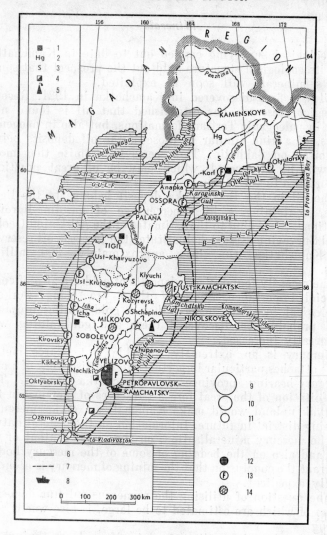

Minerals:
1. coal 2. mercury 3. sulphur 4. building materials
5. oil

6. Motor roads 7. Main sea routes 8. Seaports

Industrial centres:
9. big 10. medium 11. small

Branches of industry:
12. engineering and metal-working 13. fishing 14. timber

Kamchatka relies at present entirely on coal and oil products brought from other parts of the country. The main fuel consumer is the Petropavlovsk-Kamchatsky district (especially its thermal power stations and the sea fleet).

Of the 63 known coal deposits in Kamchatka that of Krutogorovo is the most promising industrially. It contains big reserves of high-quality coal. The bedding of the coal-bearing layers close to the surface makes it possible to extract it in places by the open-cast method.

There are several projects for hydroelectric power stations in the southern part of Kamchatka. Besides, technical-economic computations show that the geothermal springs can be used to obtain electric power. A 5,000-kw. experimental hydrothermal power station has been built near the Pauzhetka hot springs in the region's south-east. The hot springs could also be used to provide heat for the houses in the adjacent populated centres. The subterranean thermal springs in the district of the Koryakskaya-Avachinskaya group of volcanos can be utilised for the same purpose. Geologists have discovered a huge subterranean hot lake there, which could provide central heating for the town of Petropavlovsk-Kamchatsky, replacing expensive Sakhalin coal. Geothermal energy could also be made to serve more important purposes. This cheap fuel could be used in the south of the region to build up a major base for the production of fresh vegetables to supply not only Kamchatka, but the whole of Magadan Region.

The fuel and power problem of Kamchatka Region will ultimately be resolved through the utilisation of local fuels (coal in the north, peat in the south-west), geothermal waters and hydroelectric power.

Agriculture and Traditional Occupations

Kamchatka Region had become self-sufficient in potatoes and vegetables by 1958. As regards milk, meat, eggs, etc., local resources supply as yet only 30-35 per cent of the demand.

Crop and animal farming is carried on mainly in the southern districts and in the Kamchatka valley. The traditional occupations of the North are carried on mainly in the Koryak National Area. The local shore dwellers engage mainly in fishing, reindeer-breeding, and in hunting and trapping in the north of the region.

Transportation

Kamchatka Region has no land communications linking it with the other parts of the country. Its only link with the "Mainland" is by sea or air. It should also be remembered that the sea communications with Kamchatka are seasonal, since the seas washing its shores freeze for long periods (the Bering Sea for 2-4 months and the Sea of Okhotsk for 6-7 months). The port of Petropavlovsk forms an exception. Furthermore, there are no deep bays on the western and eastern coasts and all loading and unloading has to be carried out in roadsteads. From 6 to 7 tons of goods are brought to Kamchatka for every ton of local produce sent out of the region. Because of the weak development of road and river transport, communications within the region—especially between coastal areas—are mainly by sea. There are many rivers—the Kamchatka, Opuka, Bystraya, Bolshaya, etc. Only the Kamchatka River is navigable, and that only by barges and launches. Moreover, the navigational season lasts only about six months. Yet river transport plays an important part in promoting the development of the timber industry and agriculture in the Kamchatka valley. In future, when the river fleet is supplied with hovercraft vessels, transfers along the Kamchatka River will be possible all year round.

Automobile transport is very weakly developed. There are only a few roads, connecting Petropavlovsk-Kamchatsky with the nearby districts.

Seasonal transport, loading and unloading at roadsteads, the fact that goods traffic is mainly in one direction, and high wages make the marine shipping costs in Kamchatka several times higher than in the southern districts of the Far East. The building of motor roads and the improvement of the deep seaport at Petropavlovsk therefore come high on the list of the region's economic priorities. A road from Petropavlovsk-Kamchatsky via Nachiki to Bolsheretsk, to link the non-freezing port on the eastern coast with the fishing centres on the western coast, is to be built in a few years. The part between Petropavlovsk-Kamchatsky and the village of Nachiki has already been opened. A road is also to be built along the west coast from Bolsheretsk to Ozernaya, where a seaport can be built that would be ice-bound for only two months a year. The road will link all the collective farms and fish-factories on the western coast and the loading and unloading of their produce on roadsteads will no longer be necessary.

Let us take a look at the districts of the region, which are developing along specific lines.

The Petropavlovsk district embraces a considerable territory gravitating around the Petropavlovsk-Kamchatsky road. Petropavlovsk-Kamchatsky lies on the shore of the non-freezing Avacha Bay. It is the only big trading and fishing port in the region and its main transport and distribution centre; many fish-processing, ship repair and other plants are located there. It is the administrative and cultural centre of Kamchatka Region.

In the south-western part of Kamchatka (Ust-Bolsheretsk and Sobolevsk administrative districts) are concentrated most of the fish-factories, of which the Oktyabrsky, Kirov and Ozernaya are the biggest. Over 50 per cent of the salmon is caught in these districts.

The region's economic life is concentrated in the above two southern parts.

The Ust-Kamchatsk district embraces the basin of the Kamchatka River and the contiguous coastal area. The forests in the Kamchatka basin are of commercial importance. Two lumbering establishments have been set up here. Navigation has been organised along the river. The sea abounds in fish. A fish-factory has been built in Ust-Kamchatsk and a roadstead port is functioning there.

The Koryak National Area embraces the entire northern part of the region. The fishing industry is developed on the western coast. The minerals here have as yet been incompletely studied and are not being utilised. Most important in the economy of the eastern district is the exploitation of the fish resources of the Bering Sea (herring, crab). Of the economic minerals found here only the lignite from the Korf deposit is utilised on a small scale. The native population engages in reindeer-breeding, fishing, hunting and fur-farming.

The further economic development of Kamchatka Region is dependent on the growth of the fishing industry, the study and exploitation of its mineral resources, the extensive use of its hot springs and the development of tourism.

The North of Sakhalin Region

Sakhalin Region includes the Island of Sakhalin, the islands of Moneron and Tyuleni, and the Kuril Islands. Its population was 616,000 according to the 1970 census. The northern zone embraces the Nogliksk and Okha districts and also the Kuril Islands, which have a particularly severe climate. The population of these areas accounts for less than 8 per cent of the region's total.

Sakhalin Region has a monsoon climate, a colder and more humid winter and a cooler summer than the mainland. Winter lasts for seven months in the north and five months in the south. The mean January temperature ranges from minus 17.7° to minus 21.5°C in the north and minus 6.2° to minus 11.3°C in the south. In the northern parts there are frequent snowstorms and heavy snowfalls, and the temperature drops as low as minus 50°C .The summer temperatures in the northern districts are also much lower than they are in the south (+10.9° and +17.4°C respectively).

Coal, oil and gas are extracted in the north of Sakhalin Region, and the timber, pulp-and-paper and fishing industries are developed there.

Sakhalin has the only known oil and gas deposits in the Soviet Far East. The centre of the oil- and gasfields is the town of Okha, linked by railway with the port of Moskalyovo, whence oil and gas pipelines lead to the mainland.

Sakhalin supplies about 40 per cent of the Soviet Far East's oil requirements. Natural and oil gas play a major role in the fuel and power balance of Sakhalin Region and a number of districts of Khabarovsk Territory. The Okha-Komsomolsk pipeline supplies Sakhalin gas to the Komsomolsk industrial district and the lower Amur valley. It provides the fuel and raw material for the chemical industry in Khabarovsk Territory.

The forests are unevenly distributed. Timber for the region's pulp-and-paper industry is procured mainly in the central and northern districts. Because of their remoteness from the railway and the swampiness the other forests are only of local importance.

The seas around Sakhalin and the Kuril Islands abound in fish. A large amount of fish of the salmon species (quinnat salmon, hunchbacked salmon), herring, plaice, cod, navaga and smelt is caught there. Most of the fishing and processing is done in the northern Kurils, and on the western and eastern coasts of Sakhalin. Crabs are caught off the southern Kurils. There is a huge seal-breeding ground on the Tyuleni Island. Whale migration routes pass by the Kurils and the whales are hunted there by the Far Eastern whaling fleet. The waters of Sakhalin also abound in other marine resources: the weed anfelcia, which is procured in Aniva Bay (South Sakhalin) and in Izmena Bay (southern Kurils), and sea kale is collected in the shallow waters near the southern and southwestern coasts of Sakhalin.

A LOOK INTO THE FUTURE

Mankind has always tried to look into the future. In recent years an ever increasing number of works have been dedicated to forecasting the economic development of individual countries for many years ahead. In particular, we frequently read forecasts of what may be expected by the year 2000. These forecasts predict the future state of science and technology, the individual branches of production, the structure of the economy, population figures, and so on. As distinct from past centuries, when only visionaries and writers of science fiction dared to look into the future, today forecasts are made by research organisations, state bodies, special offices and firms using modern electronic computers. Such forecasting has practical aims. Looking into the future helps us find the correct solutions to today's problems.

The socialist countries have accumulated considerable experience in long-term planning. Five years has become the traditional period of time for advance planning of important economic and cultural development tasks, viz. the five-year economic plans. The five-year plans in the socialist countries are binding on all and have, in fact, the force of law.

However, to be able to establish correct targets for a period of five years, it is essential to prognosticate economic development for a far longer period. The first long-term forecast of the Soviet Union's economic development, the famous GOELRO Plan—the plan for the country's electrification, worked out on the basis of Lenin's ideas and with his direct participation—was drawn up in this way. That plan, which many foreign observers considered a castle in the air, indicated the general outline of Soviet Russia's development, and for many years tens of millions of people worked to ensure its practical fulfilment. Facts have shown that the GOELRO Plan was an instance of scientific prevision, and its main ideas about the role of electric power in scientific and technological progress and the development of the productive forces are relevant to this day.

A general programme for the development and distribution of the productive forces according to branches of the economy, Union Republics and economic regions has been drawn up in the USSR for the period from 1971 to 1980. The 1971-75 five-year plan is based on it.

In our days it is not enough to foresee the development for a decade. Modern techniques and huge capital investments have made it possible to develop vast new regions with huge natural resources, the use of which must be computed for many decades in advance. The Central Committee's report to the 24th Congress of the CPSU raised the question of long-term economic planning and long-term programmes being worked out to deal with specific economic problems. An example of such a programme is the creation of a large economic complex in the north of Western Siberia. This applies particularly to the northern parts of the country. The tapping of the oil, gas, timber and other resources in the north of the West Siberian Lowland, a territory embracing over 2,000,000 sq. km., will require an investment of many thousands of millions of rubles, and it will take no less than three decades for territorial-production complexes to form there even in outline. During that time new development problems will emerge. It is already clear, for example, that the formation of the big non-ferrous metallurgy centre in the Norilsk area will for many decades be linked with the regions lying to the south of it and the cascade of hydroelectric power stations on the Yenisei and Nizhnyaya Angara rivers, which are the biggest in the world.

In this book we have only studied the prospects for the development of the natural resources and the productive forces in the northern regions for a comparatively short period of 10-15 years, which can be predicted with a high measure of accuracy. As regards forecasts for more remote periods of time, these are still in a stage of elaboration and approbation, and the attempt to look into the remote future of the Soviet North is, therefore, no more than an attempt by the author, who has engaged in questions dealing with the development of the North for dozens of years, to make his own informed assessment. It may be that the appearance of new tasks for the country as a whole, or the discovery of big new mineral deposits, or new discoveries in science and technology will change the paths and scale of the development of the northern territories.

BASIS FOR THE FORECAST

A forecast for any part of the Soviet Union, particularly for so vast a territory as the North, requires that account be taken of the general development trend of the productive forces on a country-wide scale. The problem is so complicated that a special book would have to be written to describe it in detail, and the author, therefore, confines himself to indicating only the key trends in the development of the productive forces in the vast Soviet North.

The steady production and national income growth rates are typical of the Soviet economy. These rates will be maintained or will even increase in future. Thus, the aggregate volume of production will grow many times over. Even if we proceed from the assumption that the specific expenditure of materials and power in the production of finished output will gradually decrease, in keeping with the trend observed in the past decades, the requirements for different kinds of raw materials and fuel will grow several times over and attain a gigantic scale.

The USSR will continue to utilise minerals lying relatively close to the surface, for a long time to come. This applies particularly to the resources in the northern territories, whose wealth will for a long time seem inexhaustible. Huge reserves of minerals, notably of oil and gas, are concentrated on the continental shelf, predominantly in the Arctic seas.

The problem of utilising the natural resources of the North is linked first and foremost with the elimination or mitigation of the action of many negative factors complicating the economic development of its resources and making it more expensive. The Soviet Union has everything necessary to resolve that task. Thus, all the economic branches in the

184

North will within the next 10 years be provided with various equipment specially adapted for the harsh conditions. Fundamentally new machines, highly productive and reliable, will be operated by fewer people, and this will help radically to restructure the existing industrial centres. New centres will be formed on a new basis, their building will be preceded by comprehensive study and research and the creation of a thoroughly devised infrastructure. This will intensify the development of the natural resources of the North, lower capital investment and make it possible to create a high standard of living for the population, which, in its turn, will help to attract skilled personnel.

Major railway trunk lines will be built during the next 30 years in the Asiatic North: the 6,000-km. North Siberian railway, the 3,000-km. North-Eastern railway, the 2,000-km. Norilsk railway, and several others. They will form the "backbone" for the development of a network of other kinds of transport, which will open up vast areas for development.

The availability of gigantic power resources makes it possible to resolve the important problem of obtaining large amounts of cheap electric power and heat in a relatively short time. The solution of vital transport and power problems will help to make the exploitation of the natural resources much more effective, and considering the enormous reserves and the high concentration of the useful product in the northern deposits, will in many cases make the extraction there much more profitable than in areas further south.

All this will create important prerequisites for the development in the North of manufacturing as well as mining, even if only within definite limits. This will be promoted, in particular, by the big water resources. The automation and comprehensive mechanisation of production, notably of enterprises of the chemical and other water- and power-intensive industries, will make it possible to create, with a relatively small increase in the population figure, industries with a higher per capita output than identical industries in areas of traditional settlement. In a word, vast development prospects are opening up to the northern territories of the USSR.

Economic development forecast
for the key natural resources

We have seen that the North accounts for over 60 per cent of the forecast gas reserves and two-fifths of the oil reserves of the USSR. There are indications, however, that this is an underestimation. In particular, these figures do not take into account the oil- and gas-bearing areas in the eastern part of the Arctic zone, and especially the continental shelf in the Arctic seas. There is data to indicate that there are huge underground reservoirs of oil and gas on the vast territories between the Yenisei and Lena rivers. In any case, according to prominent geologists, the bulk of the reserves of those valuable raw materials are concentrated in the northern half of the country. This, in fact, determines the large scale and high rate of development of the oil and gas industry in the North.

Statistics show that fuel extraction in the USSR has practically doubled in the last few decades, mainly owing to the rapid growth in the production of gas and oil (especially during the last ten years). Even if the growth rate of oil and gas production decreases in relative terms (for example, because of a growth in the share of atomic power), absolute total will increase in the next 30 years several times over as compared with 1968, and the demand for these minerals in the country and for export will reach several thousand million tons (in conventional fuel units).

Modern industry needs non-ferrous metals—nickel, copper, tin, lead, platinoids, rare earth elements, and so on. Gold is now not only a universal equivalent in international trade transactions, but is used on a growing scale in technology. Aluminium and other light metals have an increasing role to play; diamonds and other super-hard materials are used in instrument-making and other branches of production. All these valuable minerals have been found in high concentrations in the northern regions of the Soviet Union, and a large part is being exploited.

There are also vast reserves of many other minerals such as iron, coal, various building materials, and prodigious reserves of water power and timber.

Until recently forecasts for the further economic development of the North were linked mainly with the idea of tapping its raw material resources in order to transport them to other parts of the country. Now, however, manufacturing is beginning to play an ever increasing role in the economically advanced regions of the North, and already accounts for 55 per cent of the total output of the European North, while its role is also growing in the Asiatic North. Therefore, long-term forecasts must take into account the inevitable increase in the share of manufacturing.

Let us look at some of the factors that will promote this tendency.

It is expedient to site timber-processing near the raw material sources, since the transport of timber incurs heavy losses of material. In this connection it is expected that a large number of new timber combines will be set up within the period under review in both the European and Asiatic North.

The prospects for the development of the chemical industry in the northern districts, especially in the Ob North and the Komi ASSR, are also great. Such development will be promoted by the inexhaustible raw material resources (oil and gas), the abundance of water, and the availability of relatively cheap fuel for power production (gas and fuel oil). Besides, it should be taken into account that the chemical industry can be automated to a far greater extent than many other industries.

The extensive development of mining, the comprehensive processing of timber, the growth of the chemical industry, which is highly power- and water-intensive, the creation of a ramified transport network and the considerable growth of the population—all this will promote the formation of many branches of manufacturing (notably of enterprises for the repair of machinery and equipment, for the production of prefabricated building elements) and the service industry. Agriculture of the suburban type will be developed, especially in the Near North, with its relatively favourable natural conditions. The scale and diversity of the economic development in the North will necessitate a new territorial organisation of production.

Areas of Intensive Economic Development and Formation of New Economic Regions in the North

For many decades to come the areas in the North where natural resources are highly concentrated will be given priority in development. In the European North these are the Kola Peninsula and the Timano-Pechora oil- and gas-bearing province, in the Asiatic North—the West Siberian Lowland, the Norilsk area, western Yakutia, some districts of Chukotka National Area, and others.

According to the present division of the country into economic regions, not a single one of them is situated fully within the northern zone. There are, however, a number of regions, whose southern parts are economically developed and who at the same time include vast northern territories which are as yet weakly developed economically. Thus, the territory of the European North accounts for over 60 per cent of the North-West Economic Region, and that of the Ob North for about 70 per cent of the West-Siberian Economic Region.

In the not-so-distant future, the above-mentioned economic regions, including vast northern territories in the stage of intensive industrial development, will have to be divided up. Their comprehensive economic development requires that efforts should be concentrated on the most rational territorial organisation of production. Until now, while the scale of development in the North was comparatively small, the economically developed southern parts of the big regions were able to take the economically undeveloped territory "in tow", as it were. In the new conditions, when the development of the North, beginning with the areas in which the natural resources are concentrated, extends to ever larger territories, where a transport network is emerging and huge power-producing and industrial nuclei are built, the position changes radically. The southern parts of the major economic regions will no longer be able to "tow" their northern parts along.

There is also another side to the matter. The principles according to which the country was later divided into economic regions (to facilitate the planning of the economy) were worked out in the first years of Soviet power. This division was based on the production specialisation of a given territory in the inter-regional division of labour, and took into account the territory's internal and external economic links, history and prospects of future development. It will be shown that the new economic regions that will eventually emerge in the country's North as its development progresses, comply with these conditions. A rational territorial organisation of production in the northern development regions will help to pursue a more efficient regional economic and technological policy with respect to them.

Thus, a new economic region—the European North—will eventually emerge from the present North-West Economic Region.

During the next three decades, the raw materials of Union and world importance—the apatite-nepheline, copper-nickel and iron ores, the big cyanite deposits, rare elements and many others—of the Kola Peninsula will be exploited even more intensively. The water power from the rivers, tidal energy, natural gas from the Yamal deposits, fuel oil from the refinery that is to be constructed in Murmansk Region, and, finally, atomic energy will be used as power sources. The first atomic power station has been built here, and a second stage of this station is under construction by decision of the 24th CPSU Congress.

Murmansk Region will eventually become one of the country's major industrial regions and, probably, also one of the biggest suppliers of export commodities.

According to forecasts oil production in the Timano-Pechora gas-bearing province is likely to reach 70-80 million tons, and gas production thousands of millions of cubic metres. The big Yarega titanium deposits will be developed. The combination of the oil production and refining with the extraction of natural gas and the processing on the spot of the condensates contained in it, the utilisation of the big chlorine-salt resources and of other chemical raw materials will involve the building of big chemical complexes. Timber processing too is to play a major role in the region's development. The big industrial centres emerging on that territory are closely interlinked technologically as well as economically. Simultaneously with the development of the above two areas in which most of the valuable natural resources are concentrated, the internal economic links in the European North will be extended. The European North will become one of the economically most developed regions of the European USSR.

* * *

In the Ob North the development of the oil and gas industry will be combined with the intensive development of the
timber industry. A large part of the oil and gas from the
Middle Ob will be sent to Siberia, the Urals, the Far East,
and also for export. The bulk of the timber will be processed
at big complexes built in the region. In the more distant
future it is expected that oil and gas will be processed on
a large scale on the spot. This will be promoted by the
building of railways, which has already begun. Most important among them is the North Siberian railway, which will
be extended from the Tyumen-Surgut railway, serving as
its first section, to Bely Yar and Abalakovo (on the Yenisei), running 300-500 kilometres to the north of the Trans-
Siberian railway.

The zone between these two main lines will be intensively
industrialised. This will be promoted by the following factors: the relatively favourable natural conditions (in the
Near North), which resemble those in the central parts of
Siberia, and favour colonisation; the great abundance of
untapped water resources, while the water problem is growing progressively more serious in the regions further to the
south; vast resources of natural gas, the exploitation of
which on the spot is economically expedient. It should also
be added that there will be links between the two main lines,
which will make for the formation of a relatively dense transport network. In other words, the Ob region, extending
southwards to the Trans-Siberian railway, is economically
most convenient for the development of large-scale industry,
notably the chemical industry. An example is the old
town of Tobolsk, where a big timber combine with
a capacity of 12 million cu.m. of timber a year, a big oil
refinery and a large complex of various associated industries are to be built within the next few years.

There are also big iron ore deposits and vast timber resources
in that territory. The future development of the southern
parts of Tyumen, Omsk nad Tomsk regions will be closely
linked with that of the northern territories in the Ob basin.

In the districts of the Ob North located in the direct
vicinity of the Arctic Circle there are unique natural gas
deposits with reserves running into astronomical figures.
The biggest natural gas complex in the world is to be built

there, and the gas will be transported over vast distances—to the Urals, European USSR, and some neighbouring European countries.

The southern part of the Ob North with its relatively big population will become an important centre of oil, gas, timber and chemical industries. As regards its industrial development, it will resemble the southern part of Western Siberia. The building of railways and the extension of air transport will establish close economic and transport ties between the northern and southern parts of the Ob North.

It can be assumed from the above that Tyumen, Omsk and Tomsk regions within their present boundaries will emerge as a new North Siberian economic region of the USSR. The area already has a clearly pronounced specialisation (oil, gas, timber and their processing), and its intra- and inter-regional economic links are also clearly defined.

* * *

In the Yenisei North, bordering on the Ob North, is the town of Norilsk, built near the big nickel, copper and other deposits of valuable ores. It will soon become the biggest non-ferrous metal production district in the world. Within the next 10-12 years a main railway line will link Norilsk with the south of the Krasnoyarsk Territory, where the Angara and Yenisei rivers have vast water-power resources and cheap coal is mined in the Kansk-Achinsk basin.

Hundreds of thousands of millions of kilowatt-hours of electric power will be produced there and a powerful set of power-intensive industries will emerge.

At present polymetallic ore is processed in Norilsk. The Messoyakha gas deposit serves as the fuel base for local industry. In future, when the railway links Norilsk with the south of the Angara-Yenisei district, a large part of the ore will be concentrated and transported to the south, where cheaper power is available.

In the Yenisei North big industrial centres will be built in the direct vicinity of big hydroelectric power stations (those in the lower reaches of the Angara and the middle reaches of the Yenisei, the Osinovo, Nizhnyaya Tunguska stations, etc.).

It is to be assumed that the formation of an industrial region in the Yenisei North will take a long time and it is therefore premature to propose that it should be made an economic region of the USSR. It seems more likely that an Angara-Yenisei economic region, incorporating also the Yenisei North, will be formed as a first stage.

* * *

The selective approach to industrial development, typical of the North as a whole, is particularly pronounced in its most remote, inaccessible and sparsely populated part—the North-East. Only the gradual economic development of individual districts in the North-East will create conditions for economic links between them. The nuclear-type development is particularly evident in the North-East (the Yakut ASSR, and Magadan and Kamchatka regions).

The huge industrial development tasks facing the Yakut ASSR and Magadan Region in the next decade raise the question of the expediency of making this area an independent economic region. The Yakut ASSR and Magadan Region, in perspective also the northern part of Kamchatka Region, are characterised by a more or less identical specialisation in the all-Union division of labour (the extraction of valuable metals and minerals, and ones that are in short supply) which will doubtlessly continue for many years to come. At the same time, the regions of the North-East possess all the conditions for the creation of a fuel and power base of their own, and they could become self-sufficient in timber, vegetables, potatoes and meat, and also building materials, which are at present brought in over vast distances.

One of the most important problems connected with the formation of an integrated economic region in the North-East of the USSR is the creation of main transport arteries, the "backbone" for future transport network. In the western part of the territory this has already emerged. The Lena River, and the permanent and winter roads, radiating from it, and the Osetrovo-Ust-Kut railway, provide a transport distribution network in that area. The communications network based on the Lena River and the Northern Sea Route embraces the entire western and northern parts of the North-East and is of paramount importance to the development of the economic links between the industrial centres in that territory.

In the eastern districts, the North-Eastern railway will eventually provide a similar transport axis. Linked with the

192

system of the Lena waterways, it will form the "backbone" of a unified transport system in the North-East.

The formation of a single transport network in the North-East of the USSR should also involve linking up the North-Eastern railway and the navigable parts of the Yana, Indigirka and Kolyma rivers. This will make it possible to combine freight transfers along the Northern Sea Route with freight transfers by rail.

The above main arteries, together with the internal transport network of every district, will embrace the whole territory of the North-East. They will be supplemented by a network of air routes.

The formation of an integrated economic region in the North-East also requires the setting up of a network of fuel and power bases. Of great importance in this connection is the utilisation of the natural gas deposits in the basin of the Vilyui River. Atomic power stations will play an important role in the production of relatively cheap electric power. Plans also provide for the building of hydroelectric power stations.

All the above shows that industrial development will be stepped up in the North-East in future.

* * *

The USSR has larger northern territories than any other country, and economic development has assumed a corresponding scale. In time these regions will become increasingly important to the Soviet Union's economy because the tapping and utilisation of the natural resources of the North can contribute to the solution of a number of fundamental problems of the Soviet Union's long-term economic development.

The exclusive wealth of the Soviet Union's northern territories, the unique concentration of such minerals as oil and gas, diamonds, non-ferrous and rare metals, the re-equipment of all economic branches in the North with more productive equipment now under way, and the policy of reducing labour costs to a minimum and various other measures will all serve to make the development of the North economically effective. The development of the North is an organic part of the long-term development plans for the country as a whole.

REQUEST TO READERS

Progress Publishers would be glad to have your opinion of this book, its translation and design.

Please send your comments to 21, Zubovsky Boulevard, Moscow, USSR.

PREGRESS PUBLISHERS WILL SOON PUBLISH

POKSHISHEVSKY V.
Geography of the Soviet Union.
Its Nature, Population, Economy and Regions

This book provides a detailed economic and geographical description of the Soviet Union. Much space
is given to the history of its economic progress, the
development of regional-territorial and production
complexes, the distribution of the population and urba-
nisation. The reader is given a great deal of information
about the regions of the country, their geographical
features, resources and the tasks of economic development
they face. The book contains basic data on economic
development by branches and is supplemented with
charts, diagrams, tables and reference material describing
land structure, natural resources and the composition of
the population in the regions.

RYABININ B.
Across the Urals

The author has travelled widely in the Urals. He climbed the tallest mountains, went down into the caves, rambled in the forests, and sailed the rivers. He gives an entertaining account of his wanderings, and speaks of the scenery, the peculiarities and riddles of the Urals in a very interesting manner.

The Urals are impressively beautiful. But no less impressive is the feat of the people who had developed this forbidding mountainous country stretching for more than two thousand kilometres from the Arctic Ocean down to the Kazakh steppes. Soviet geologists are discovering more and more of its fabulous mineral wealth, and the author speaks of the striking changes which have taken place here in the years of Soviet power, telling a fascinating story about the builders of the giant industrial enterprises which have completely transformed the scenery and life of the Urals.

Soviet Georgia

The Colchis lowlands where palms and eucalyptus trees thrive, the slopes of the Caucasian mountains clothed in dense pine woods and crowned by the extinct volcanoes Kazbek and Elbrus, the arid steppes of the Iori plateau, and the lush vineyards in the Alazani valley, are all features of Georgia's landscape. The author of this book gives a vivid description of the country's scenic beauties, dwells on its history, its ancient and highly developed culture, and its modern multibranch economy.

The widest circle of readers will enjoy this informative and popularly written book.

Soviet Armenia

Soviet Armenia is not a large country, but it has great natural wealth and a developed economy. It is also a land of ancient culture which has produced unsurpassable examples of architecture, literature, art and music. Armenia's contribution to the Soviet Union's integrated economy is quite substantial.

This book will give you an exhaustive idea of this attractive land.